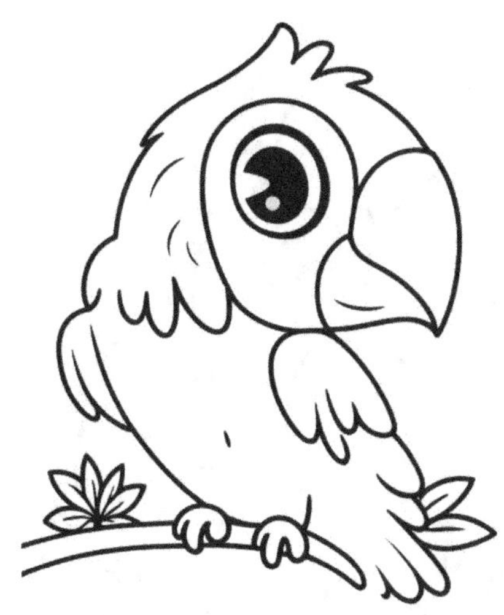

For all the creative and curious children out there, who bring color and joy to the world with their imagination. May this coloring book be a blank canvas for your brightest dreams and your most colorful adventures. May each stroke and every color bring a smile to your face and inspire new stories. May art accompany you on all journeys of life. Have fun coloring!

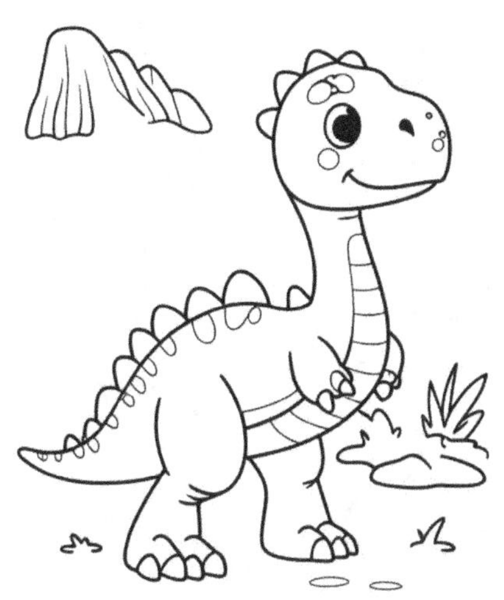

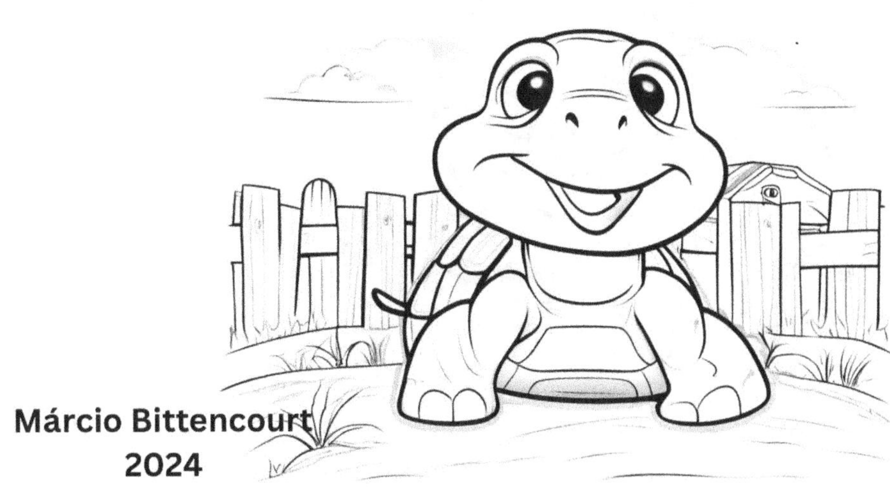

Márcio Bittencourt
2024

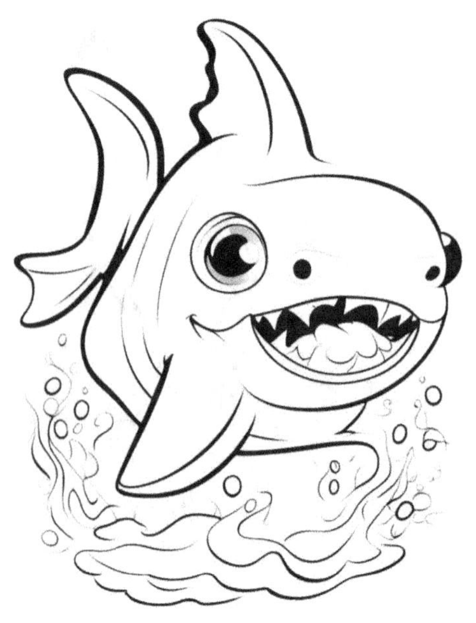
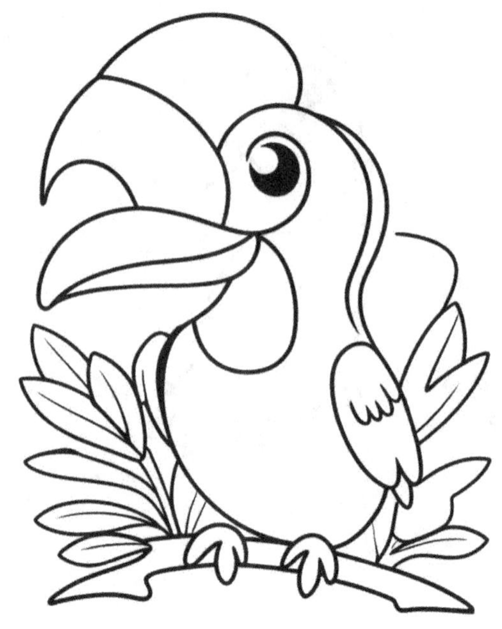

This Book Belongs To:

____

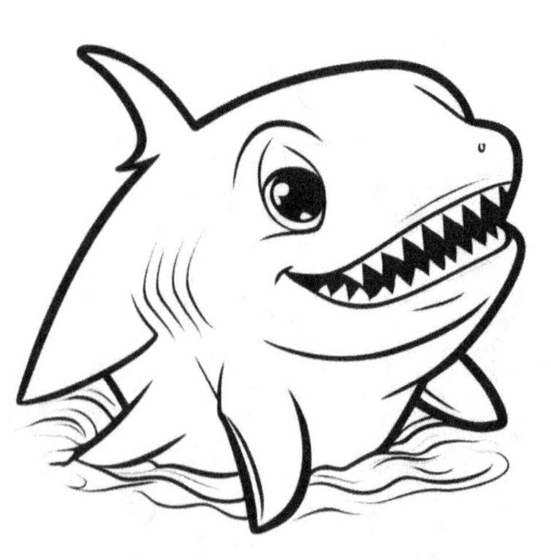
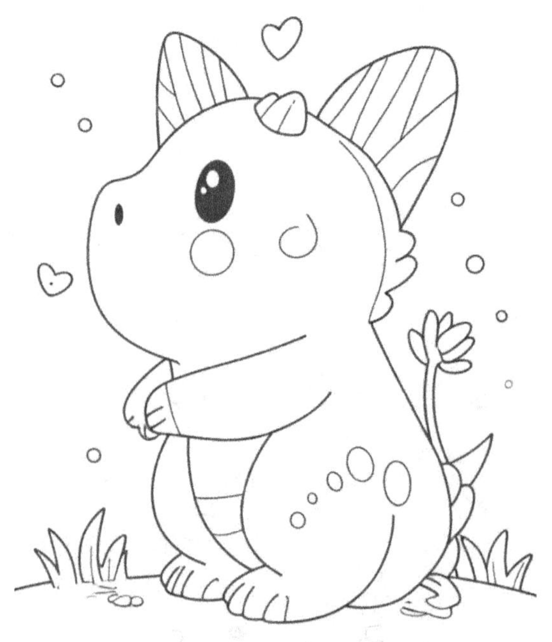

Test Color Page.

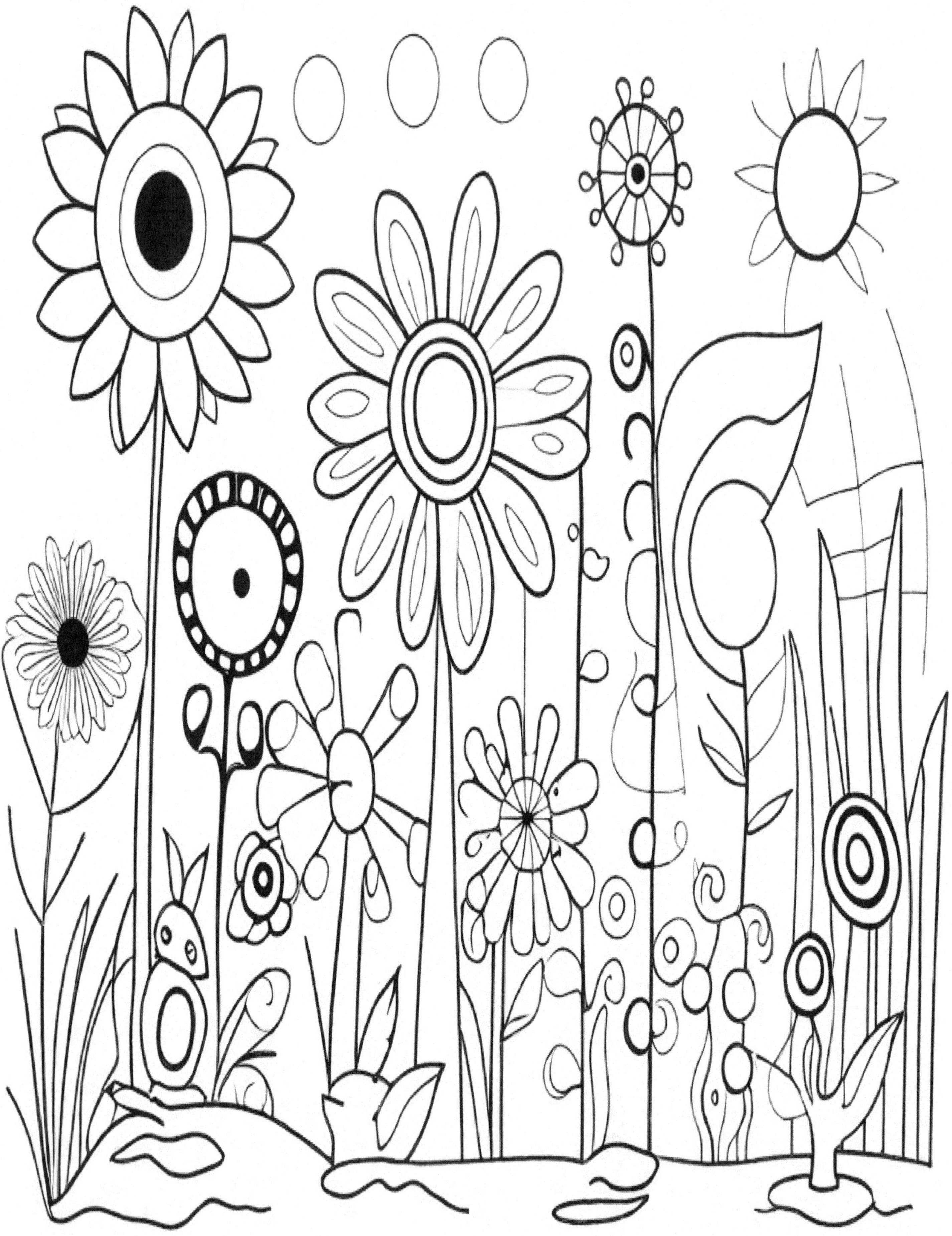

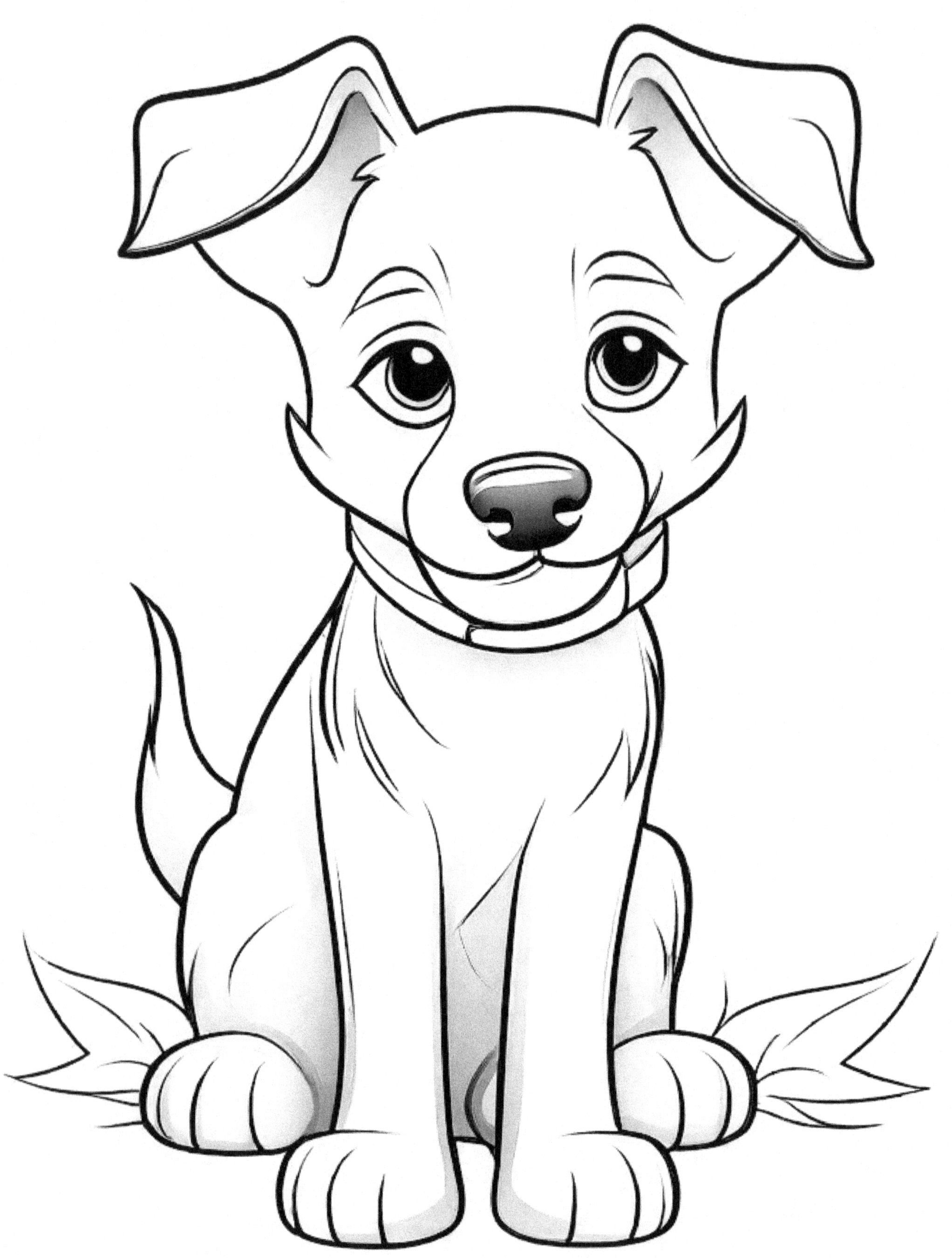

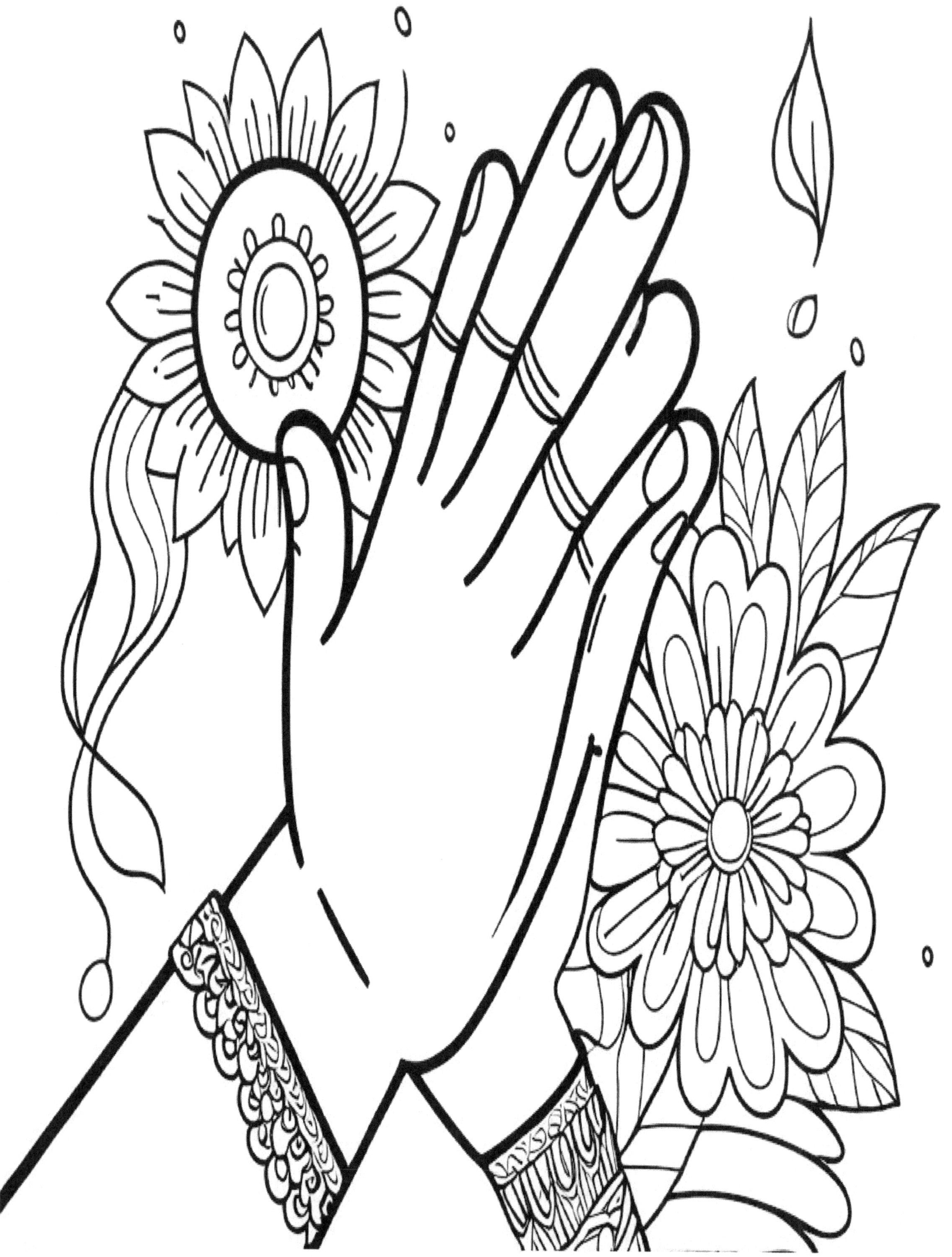

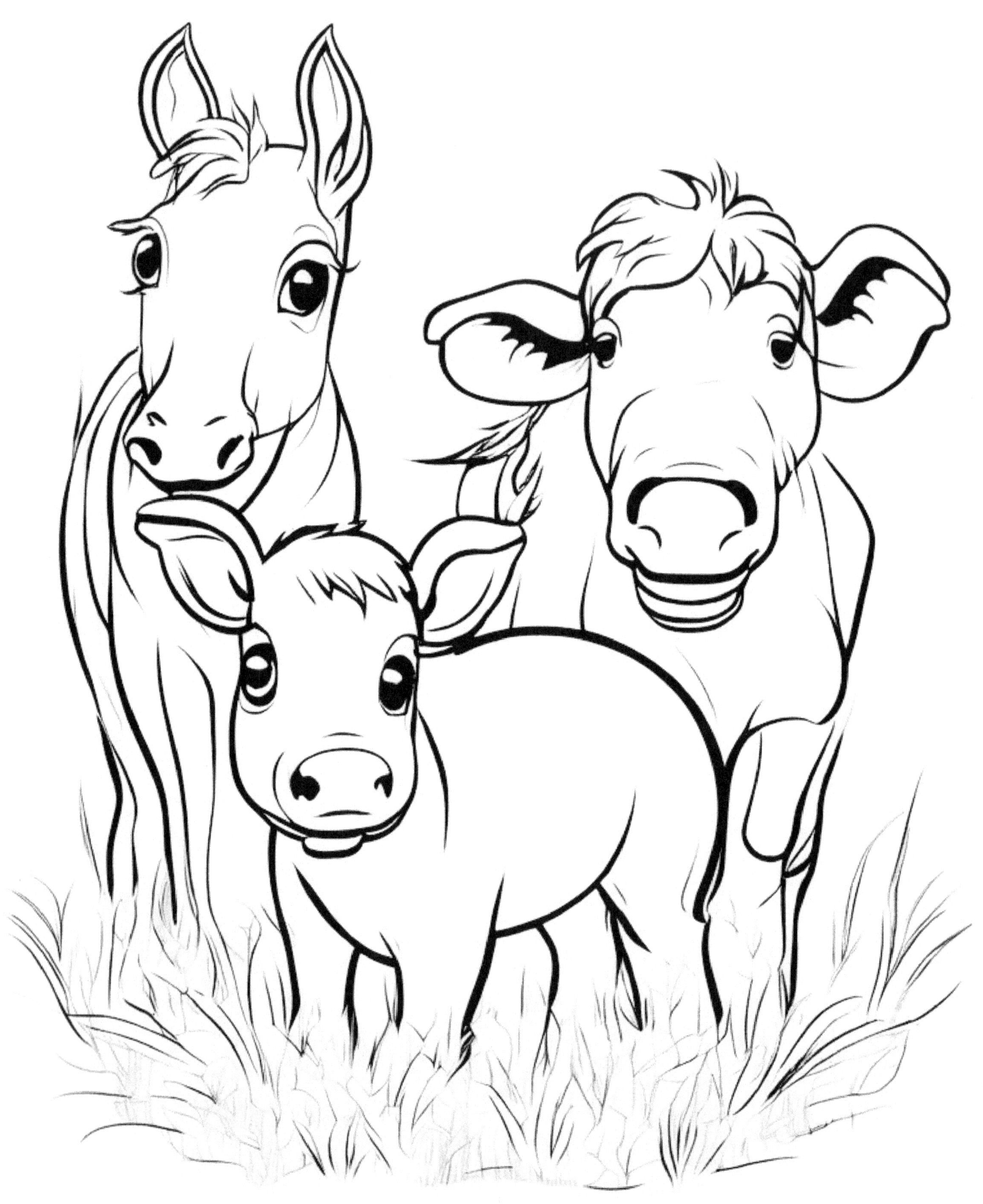

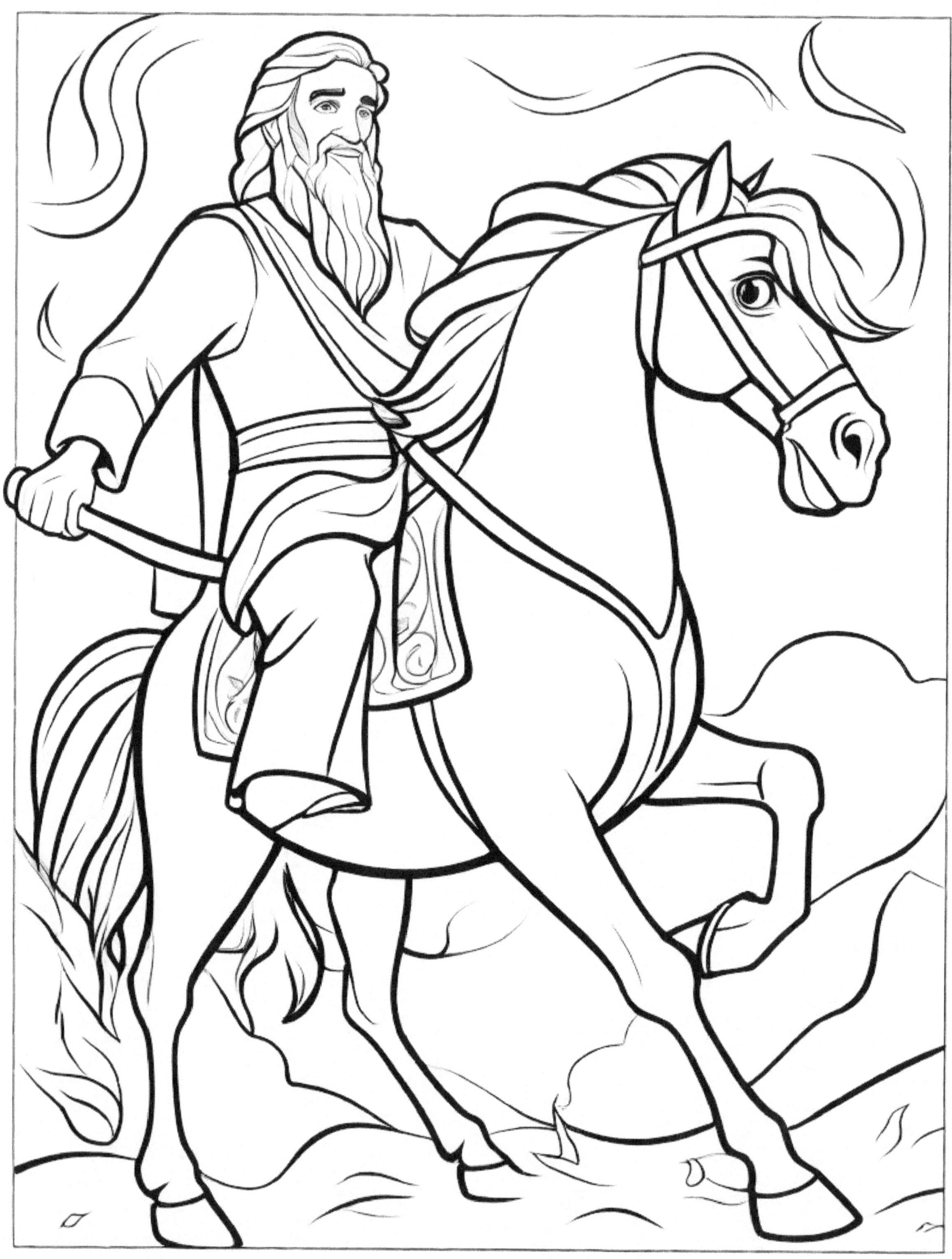

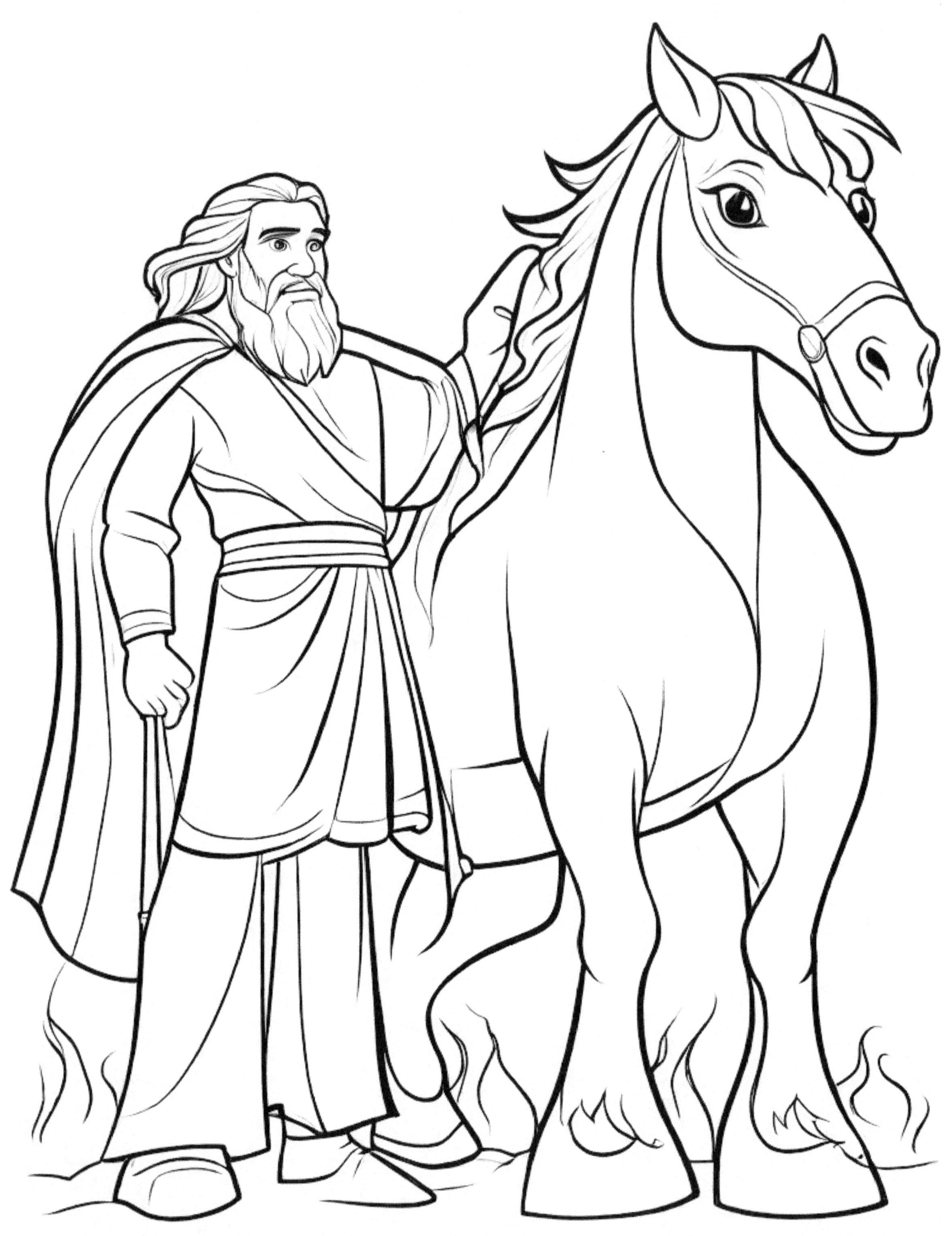

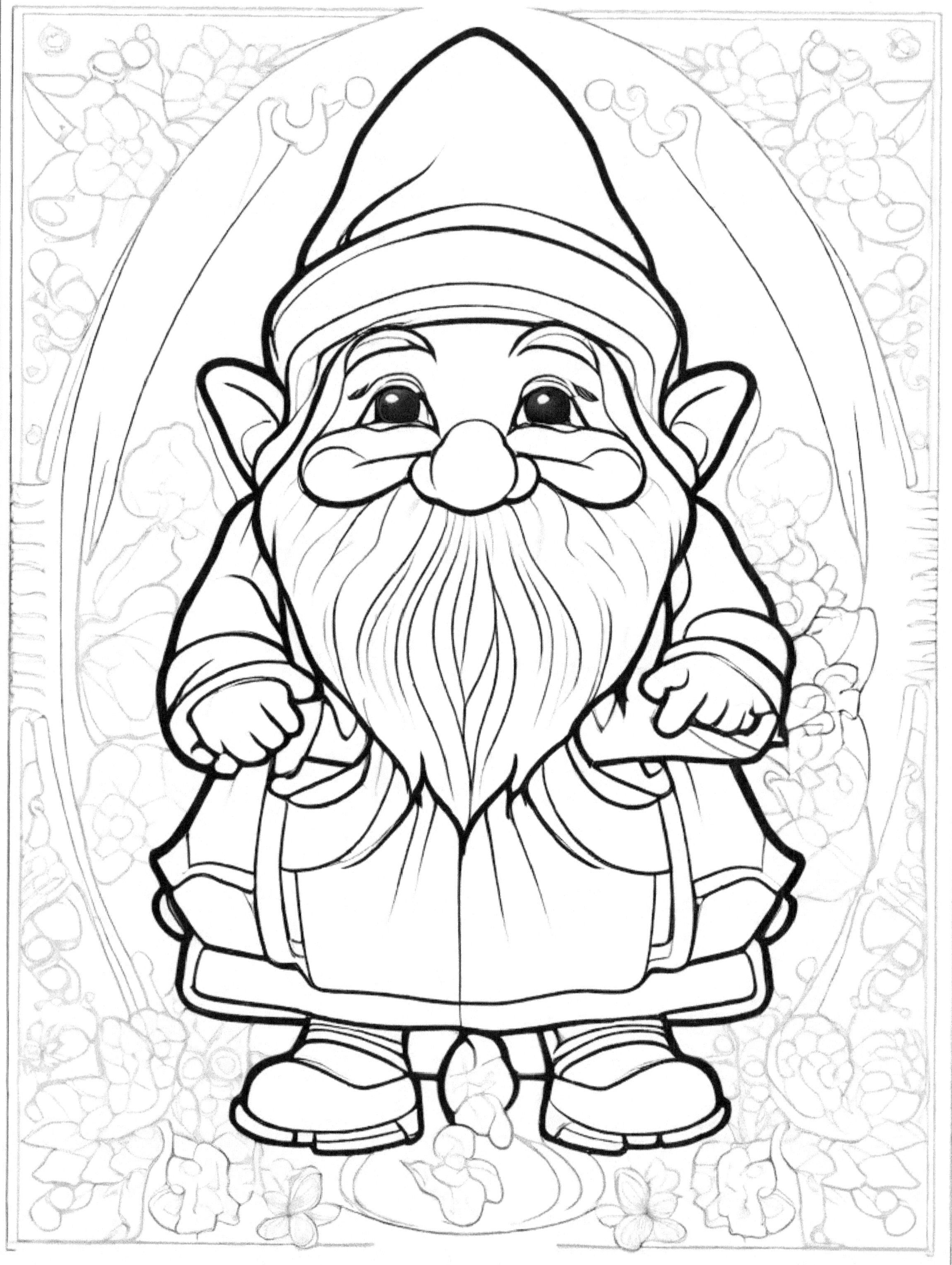

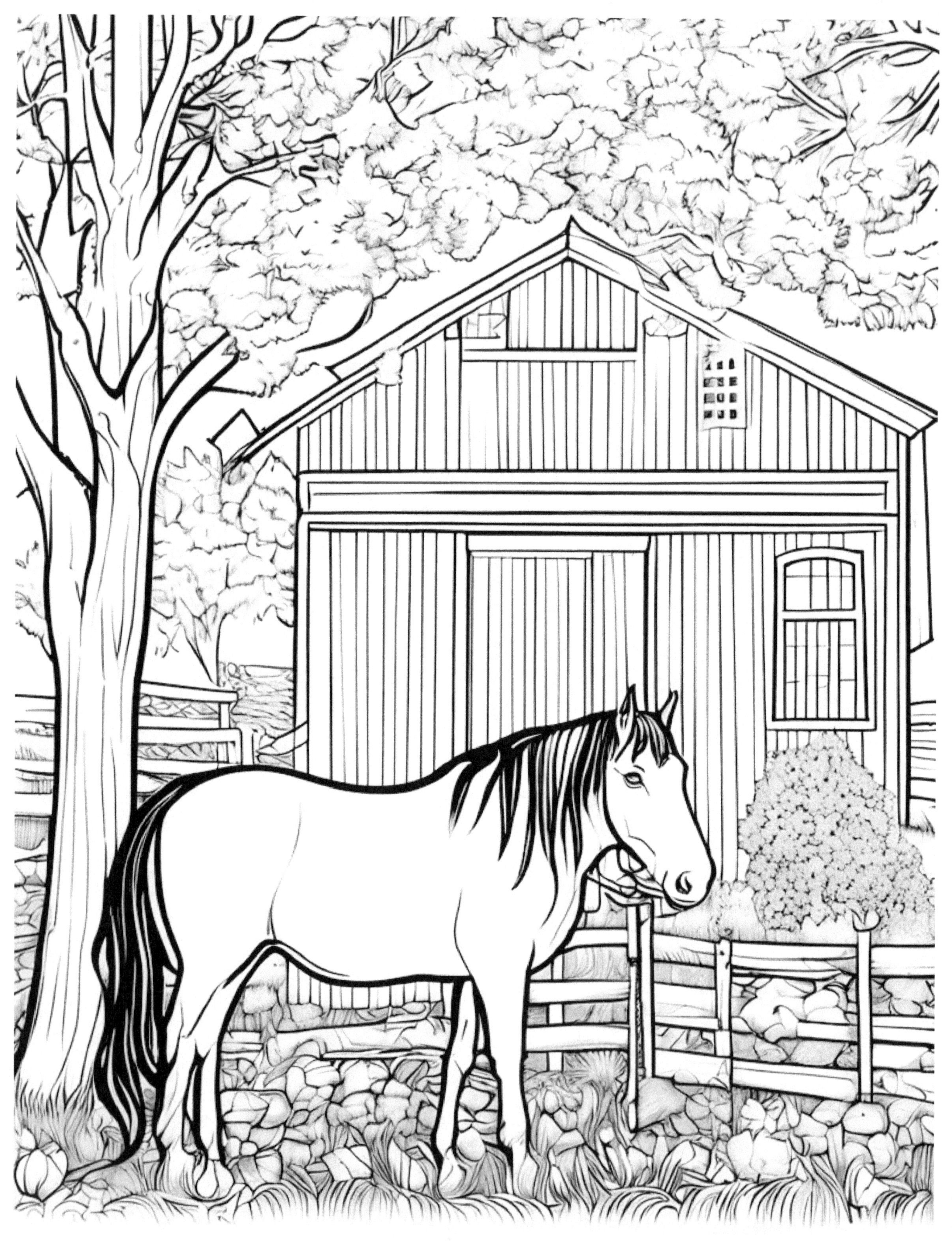

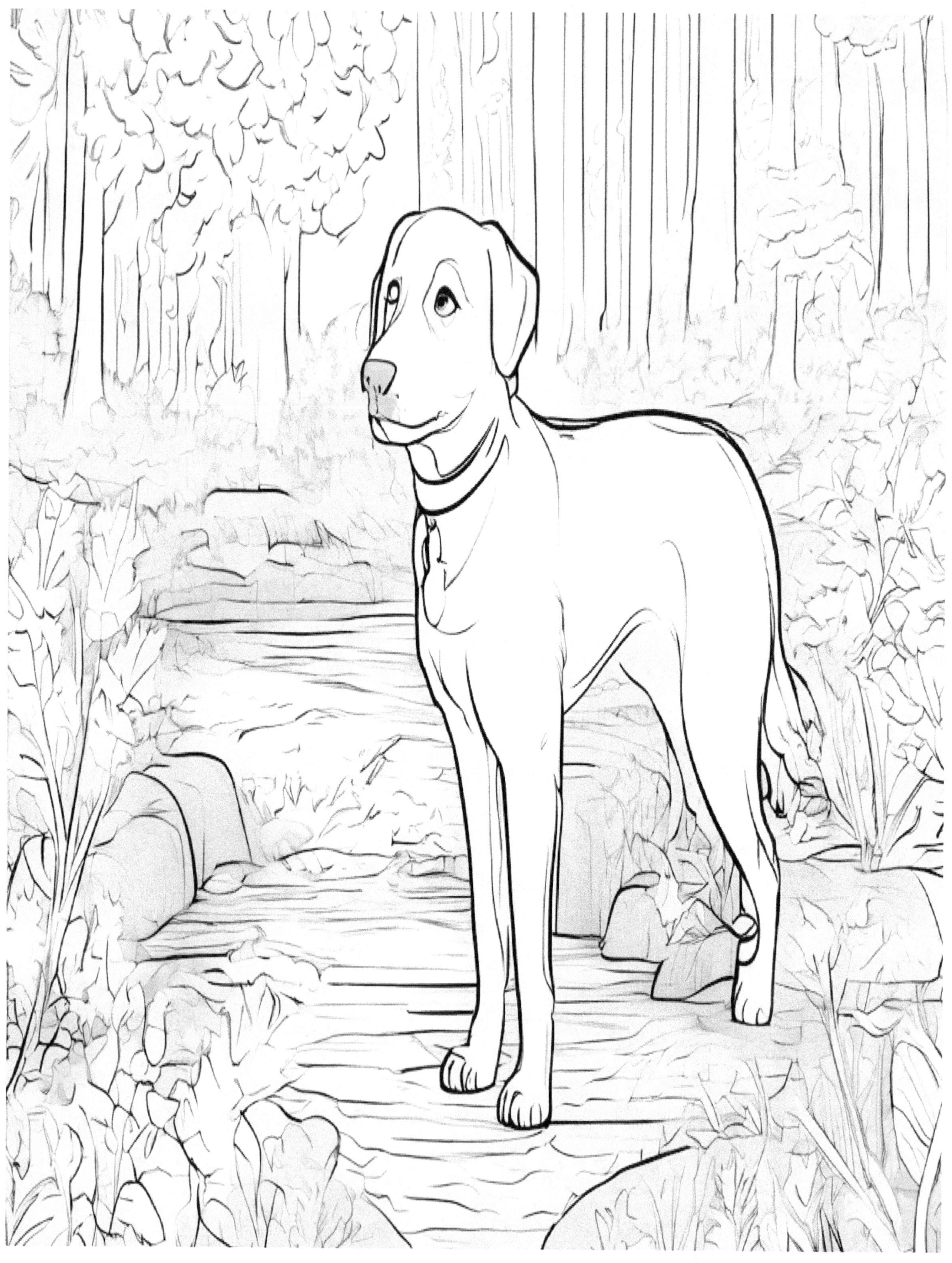

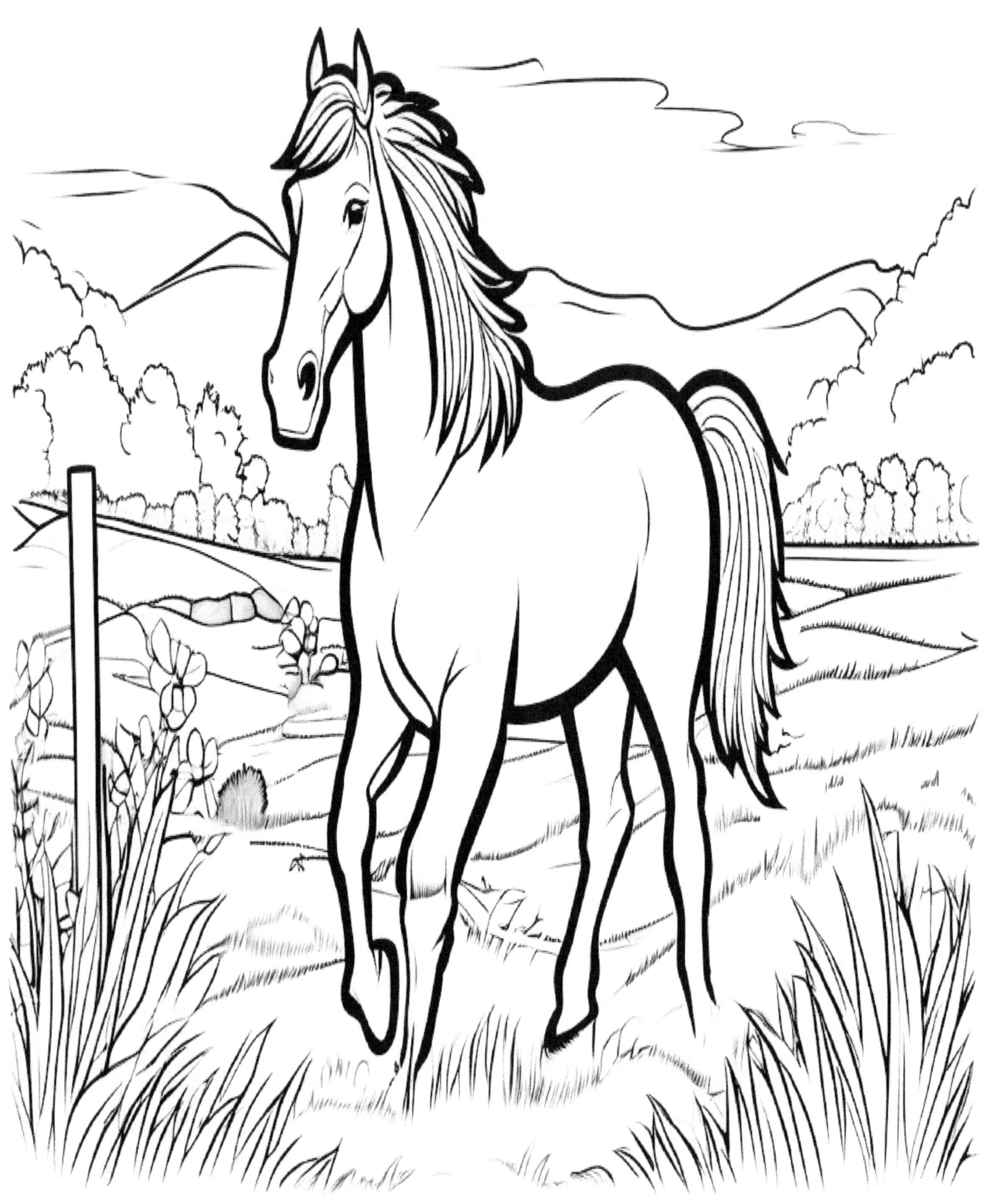

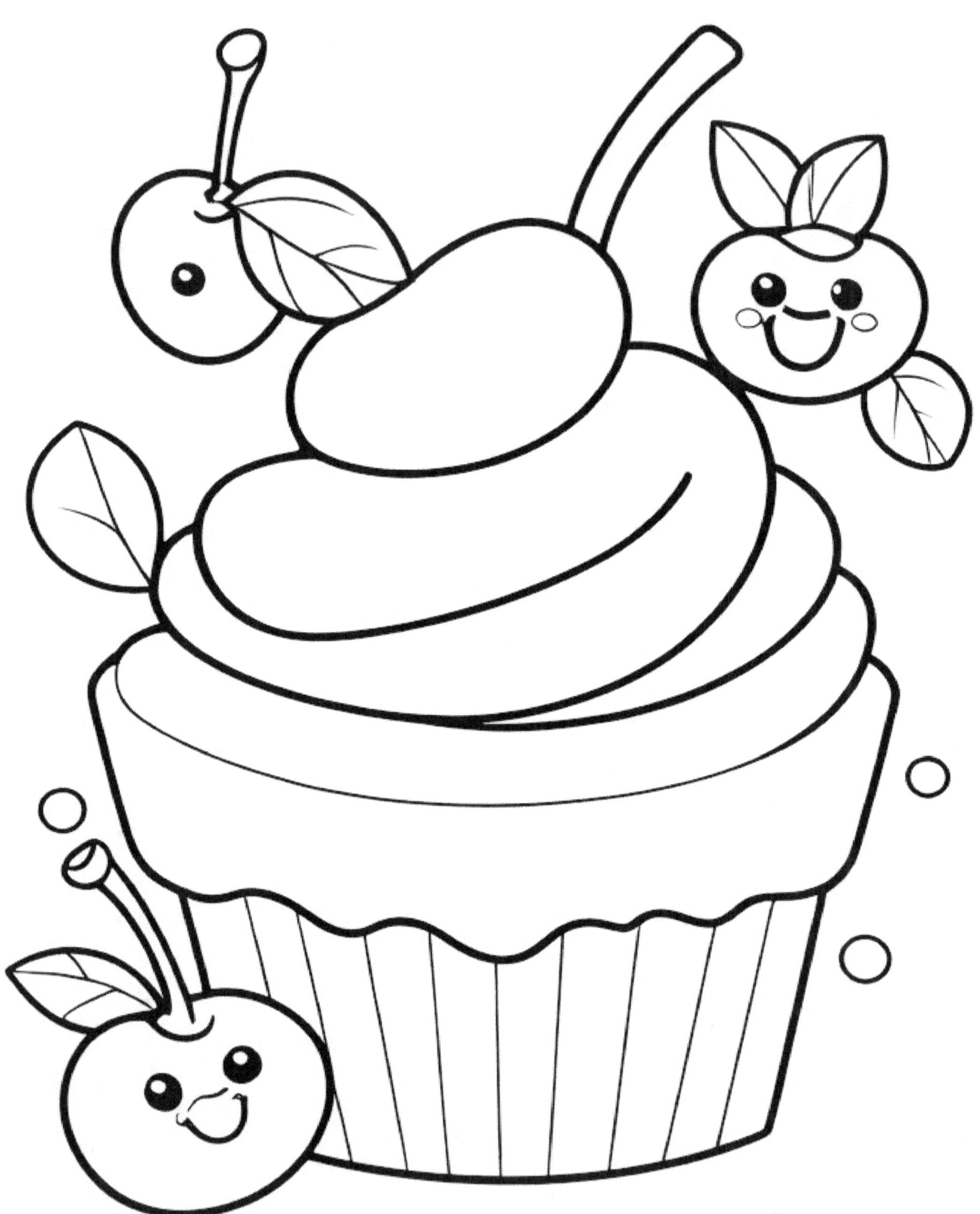

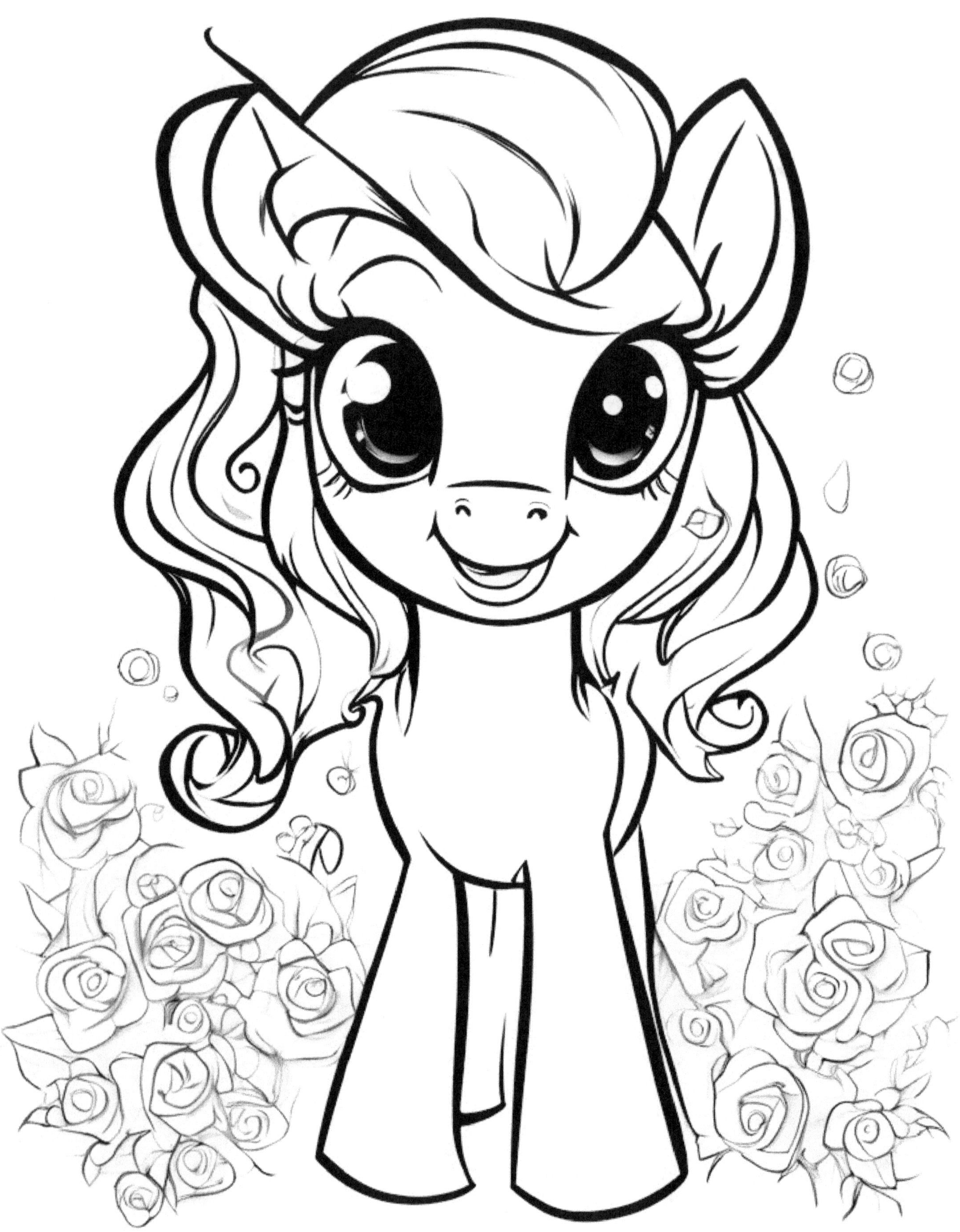

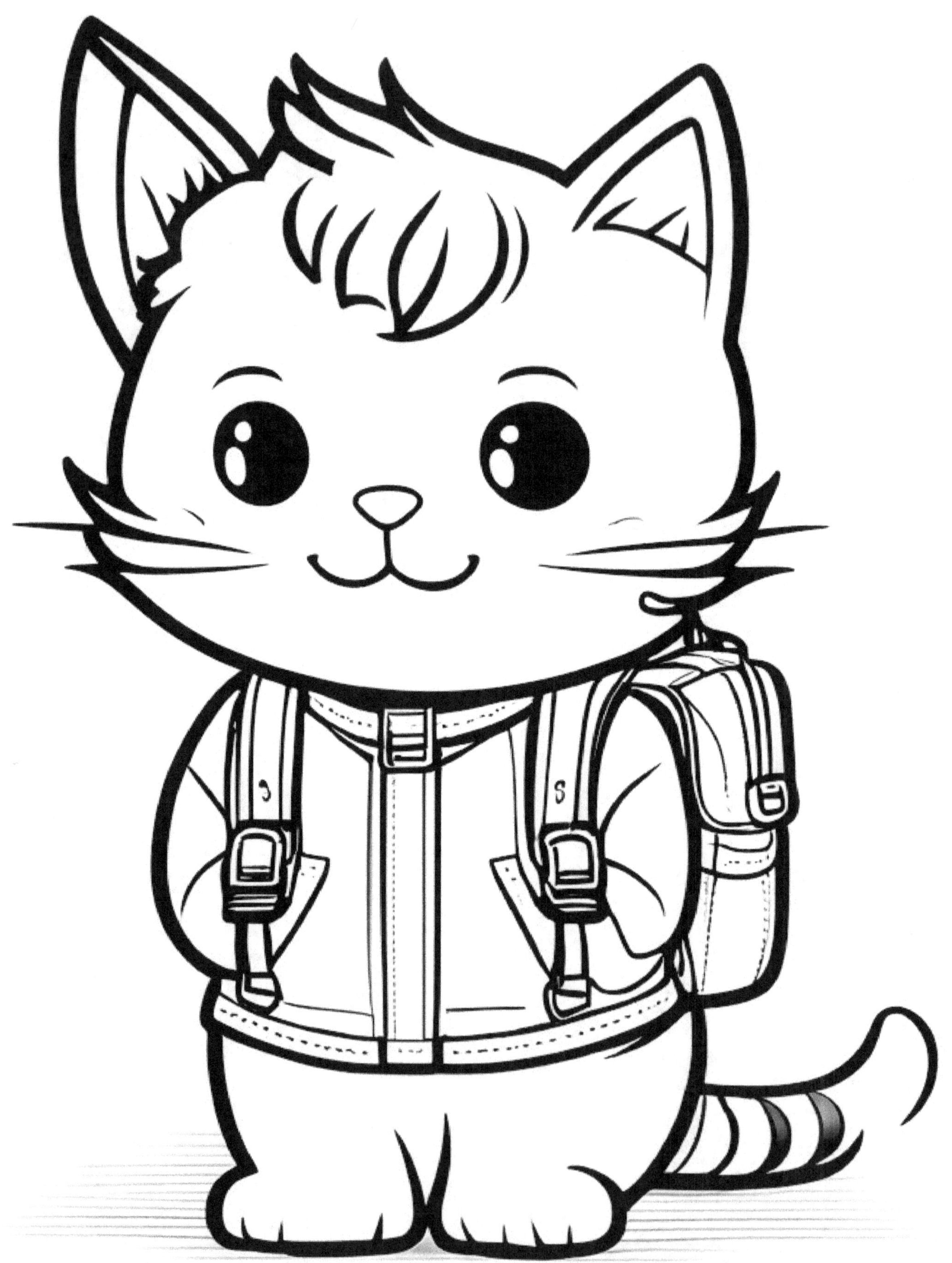

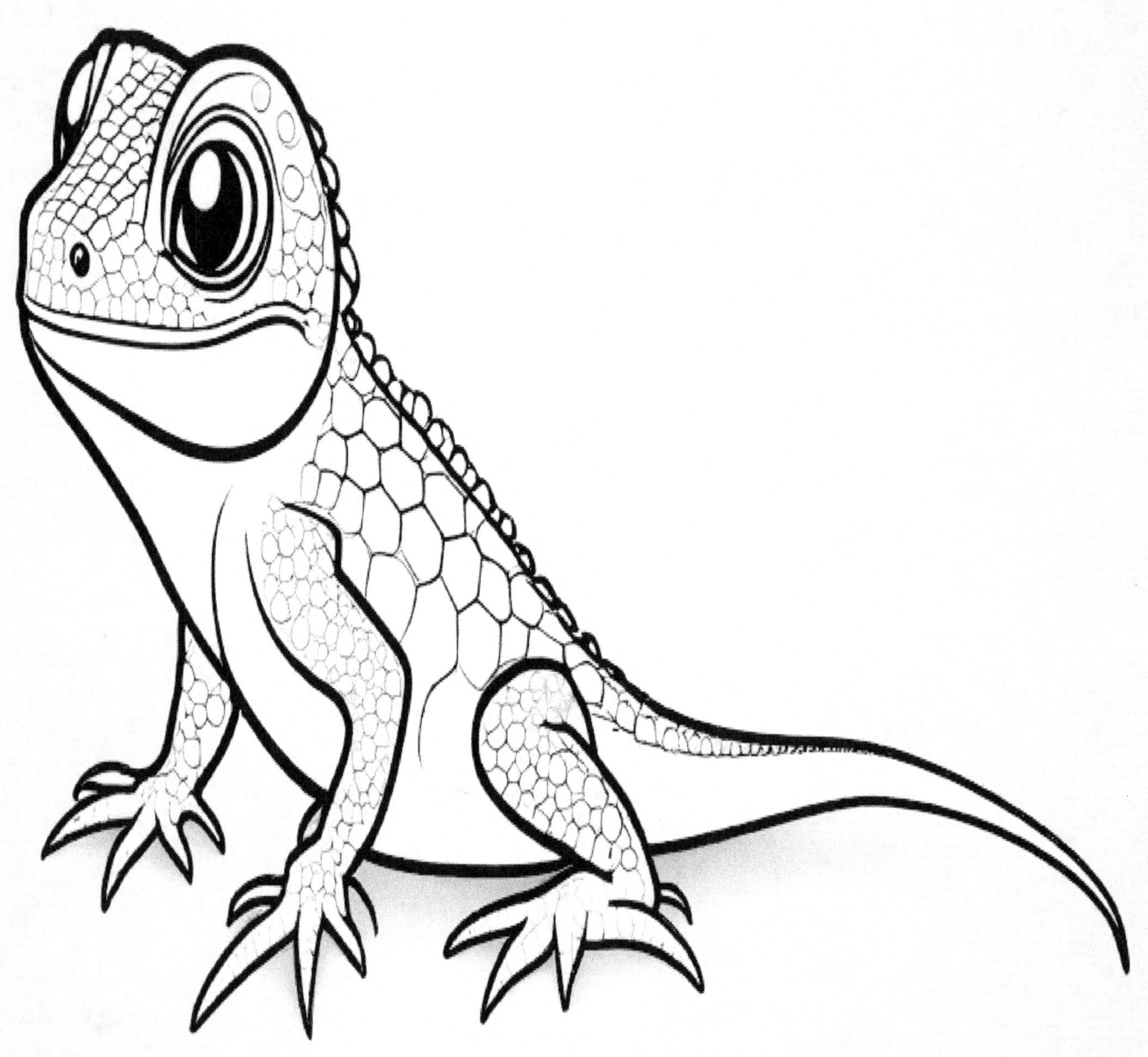

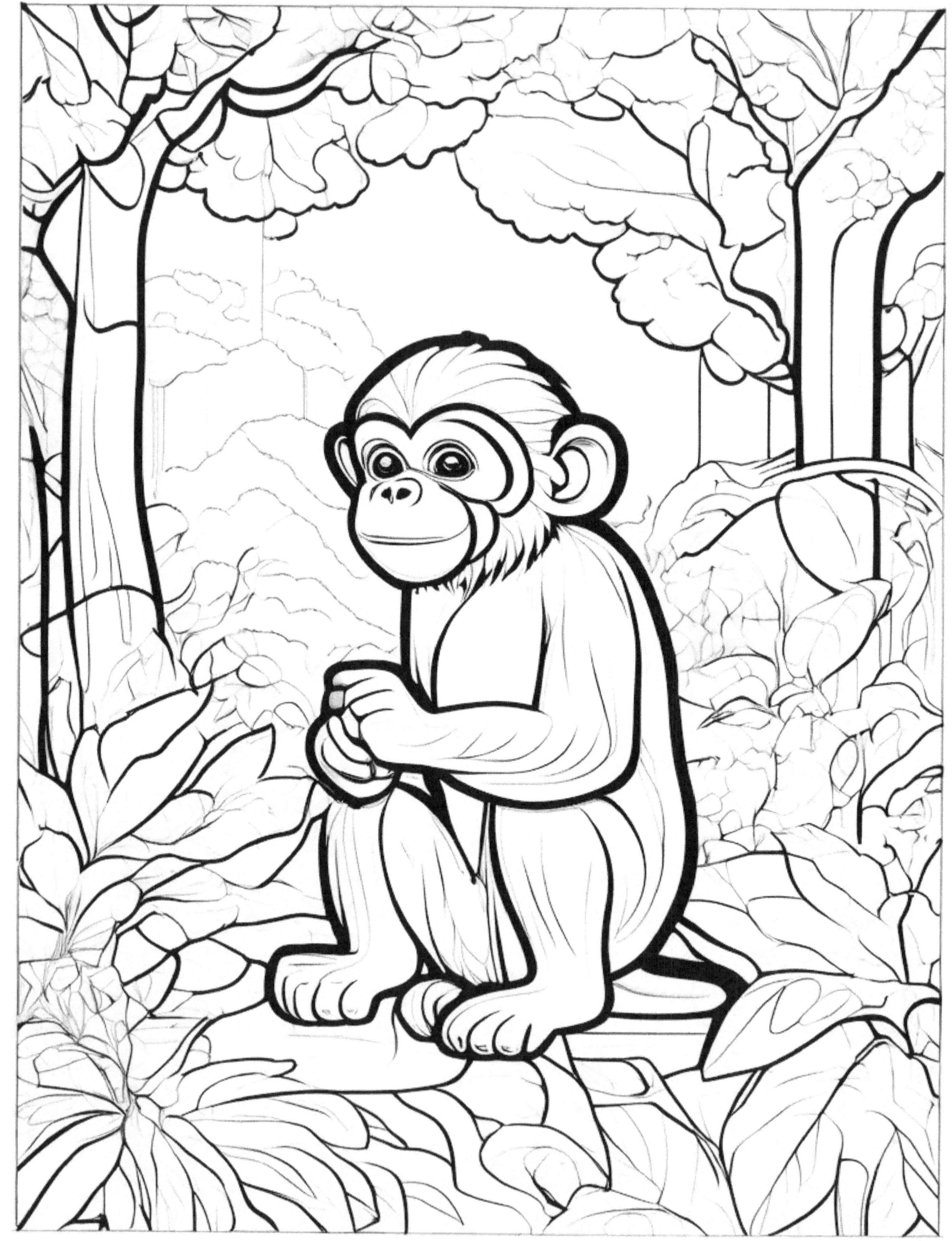

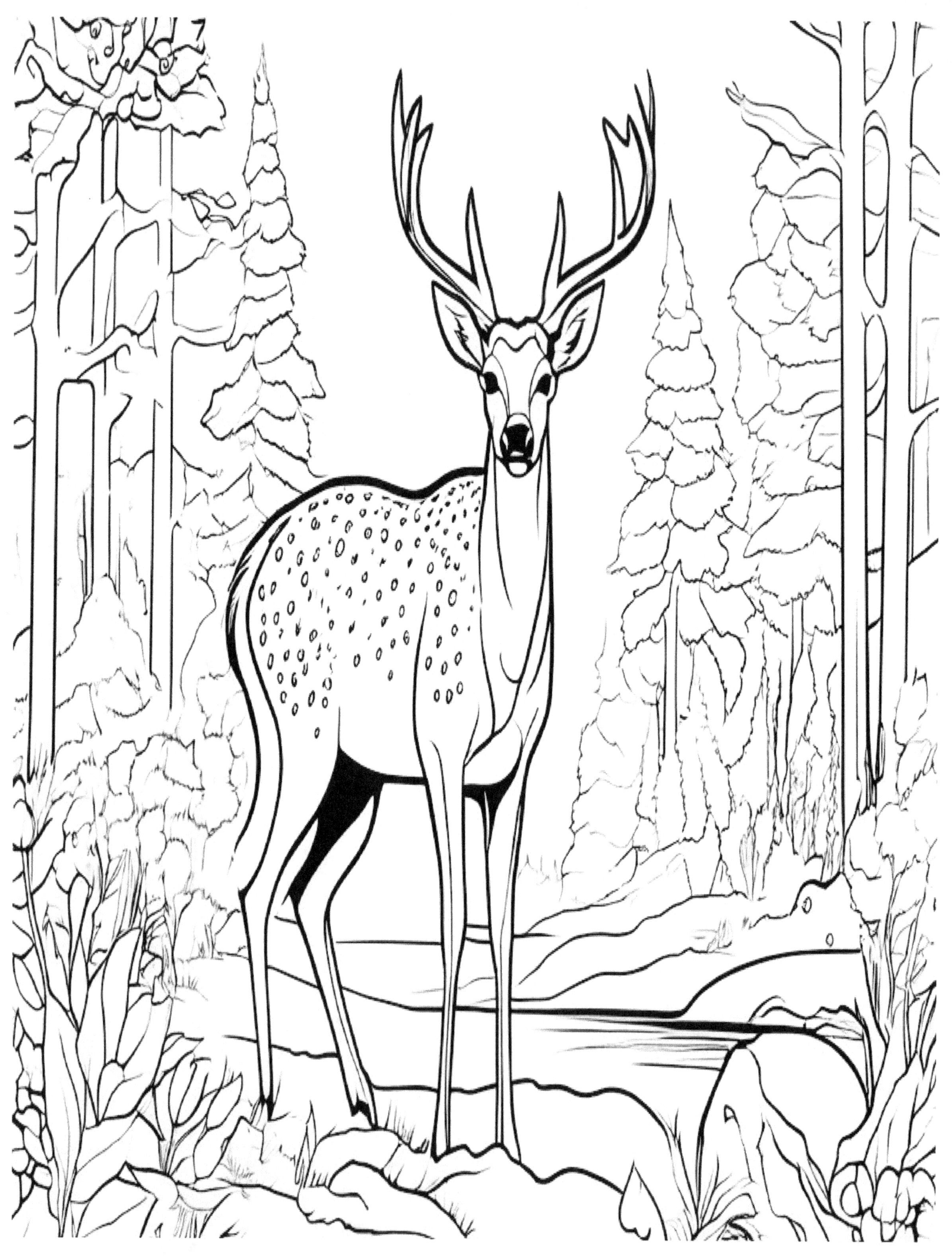

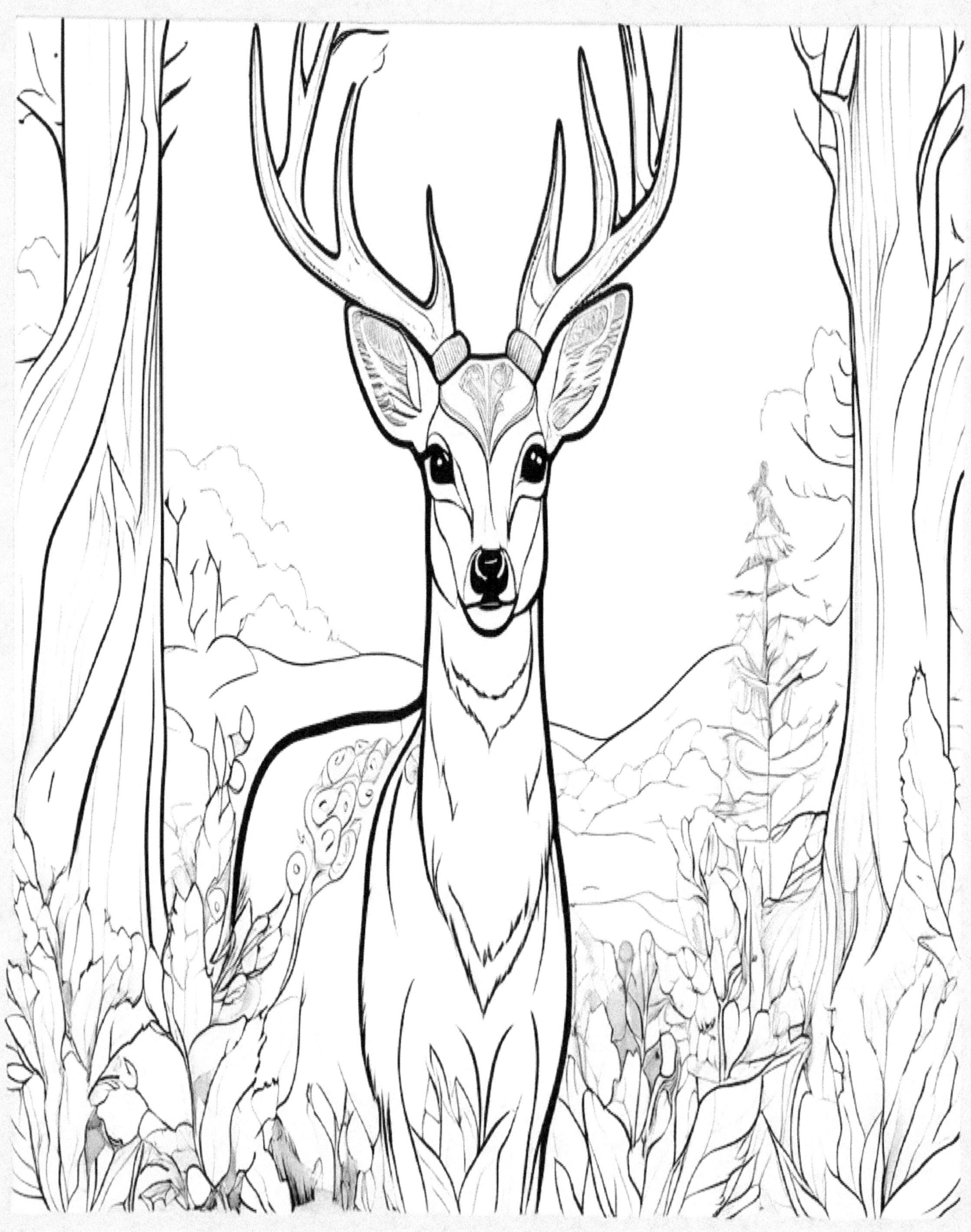

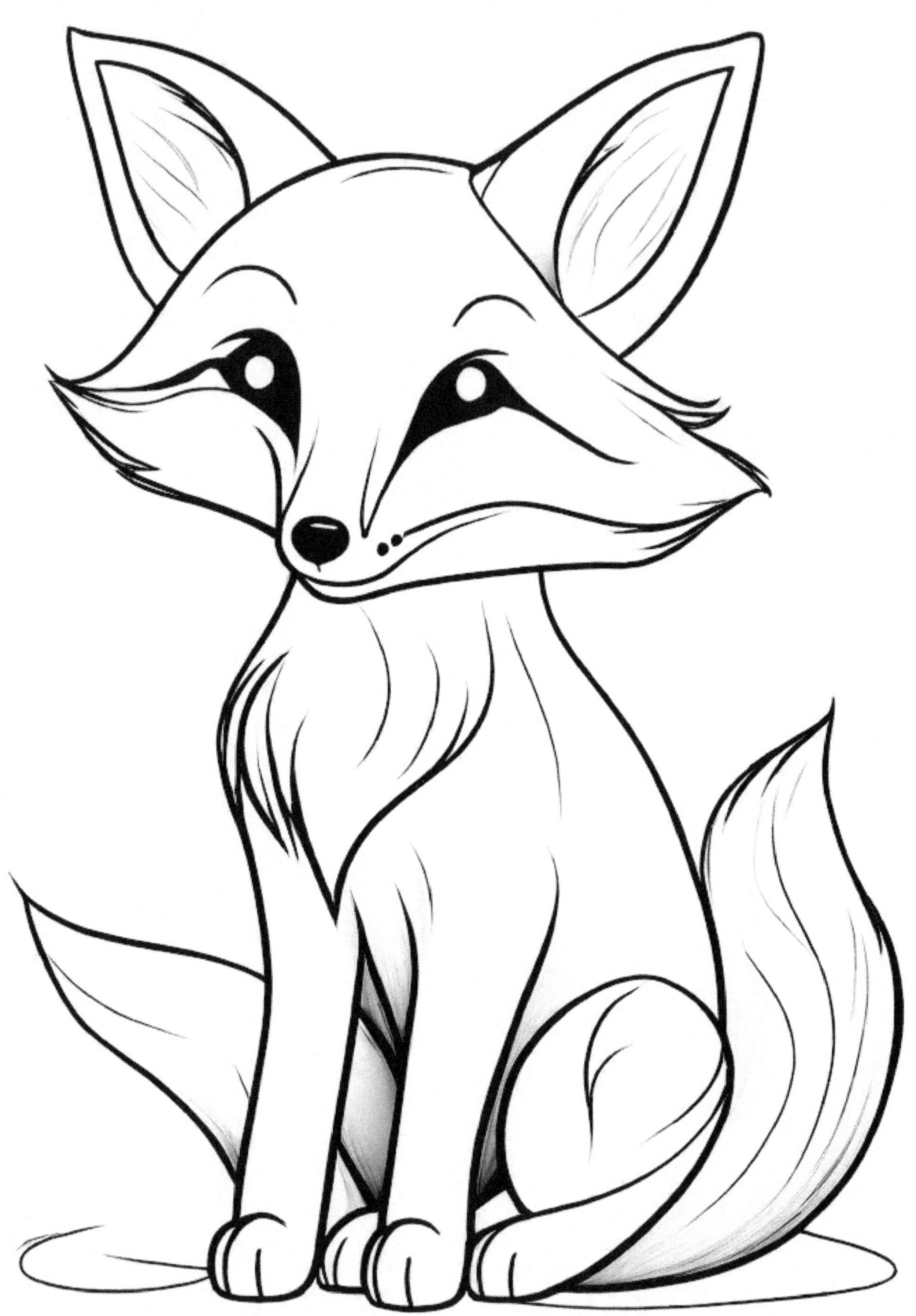

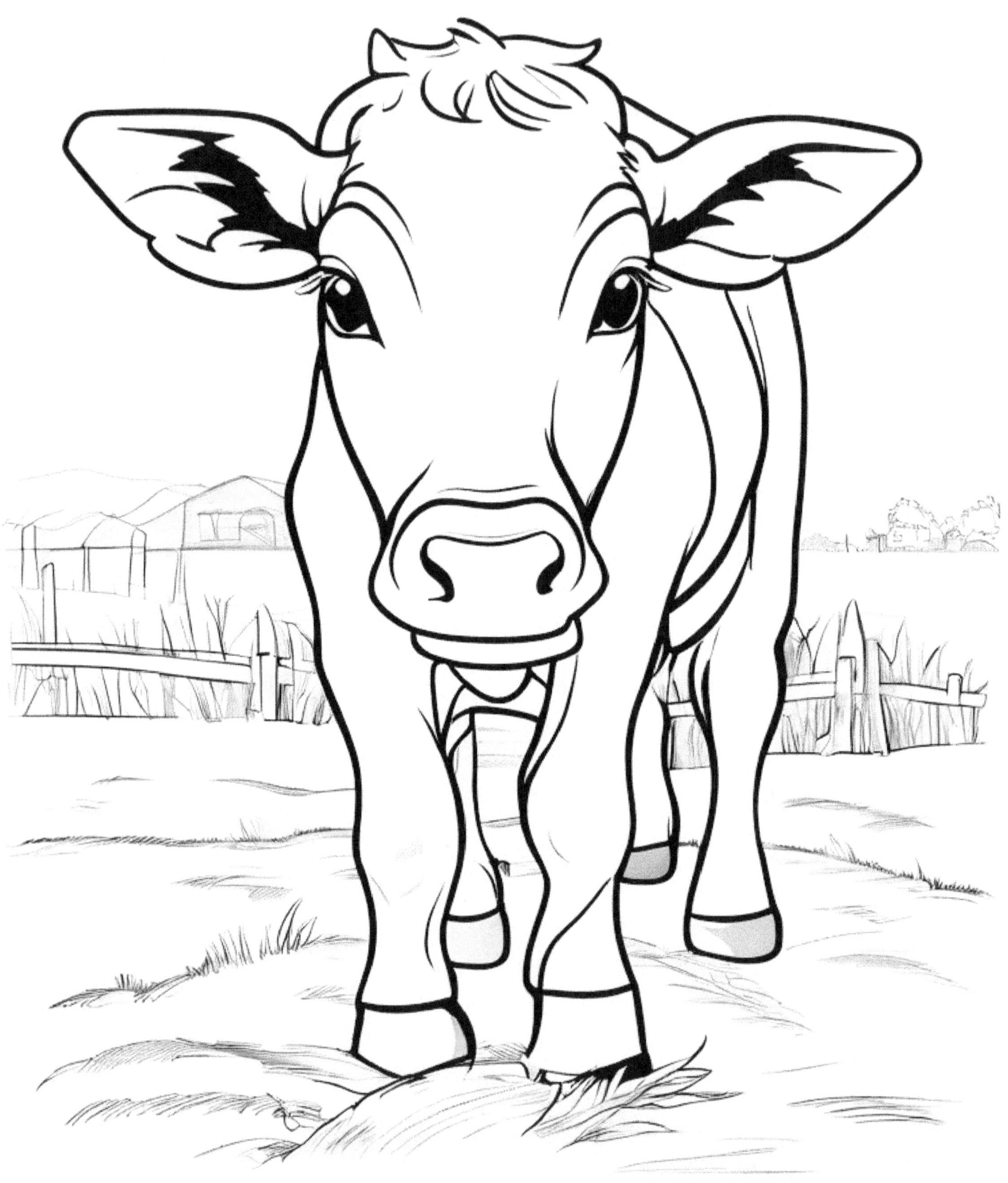

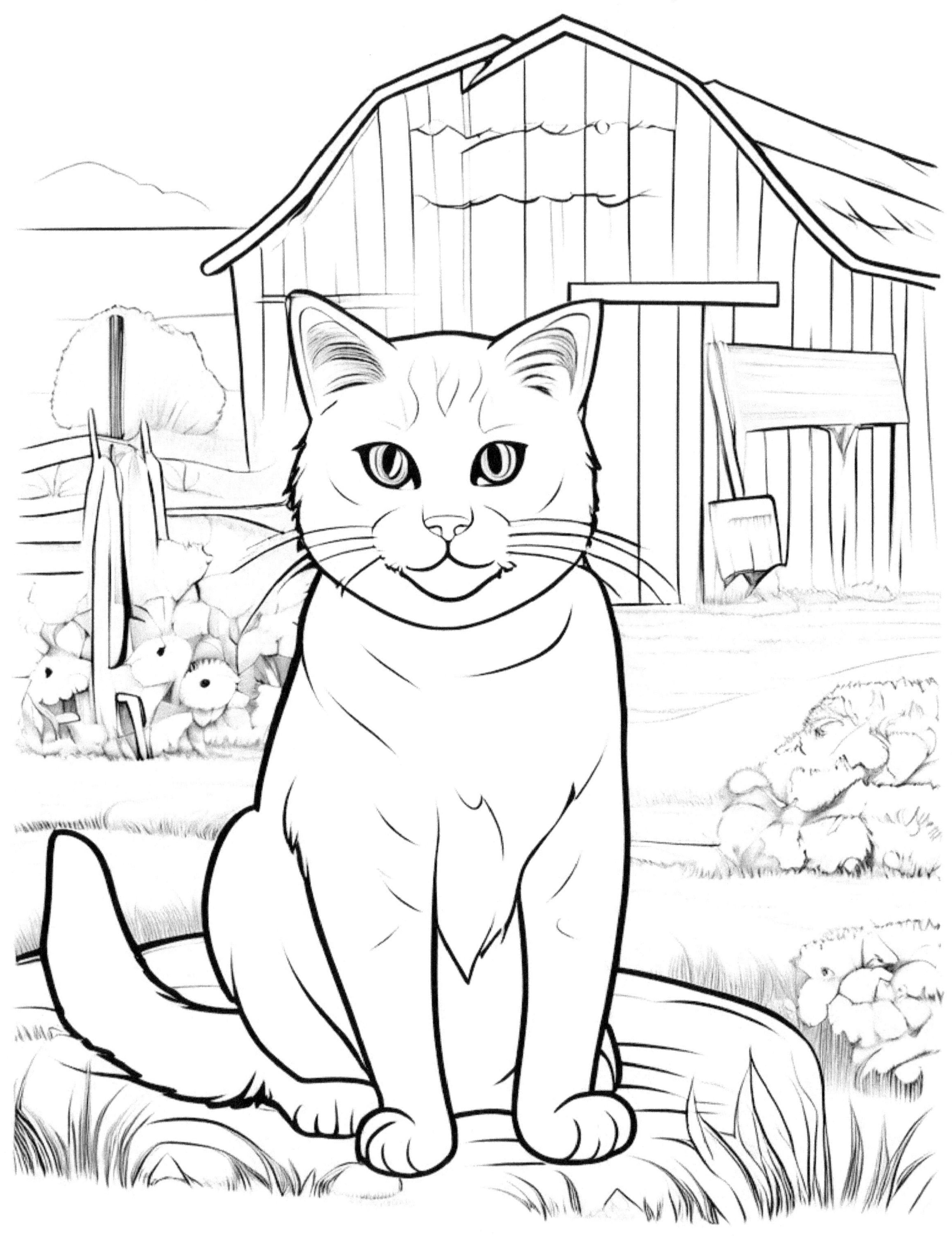

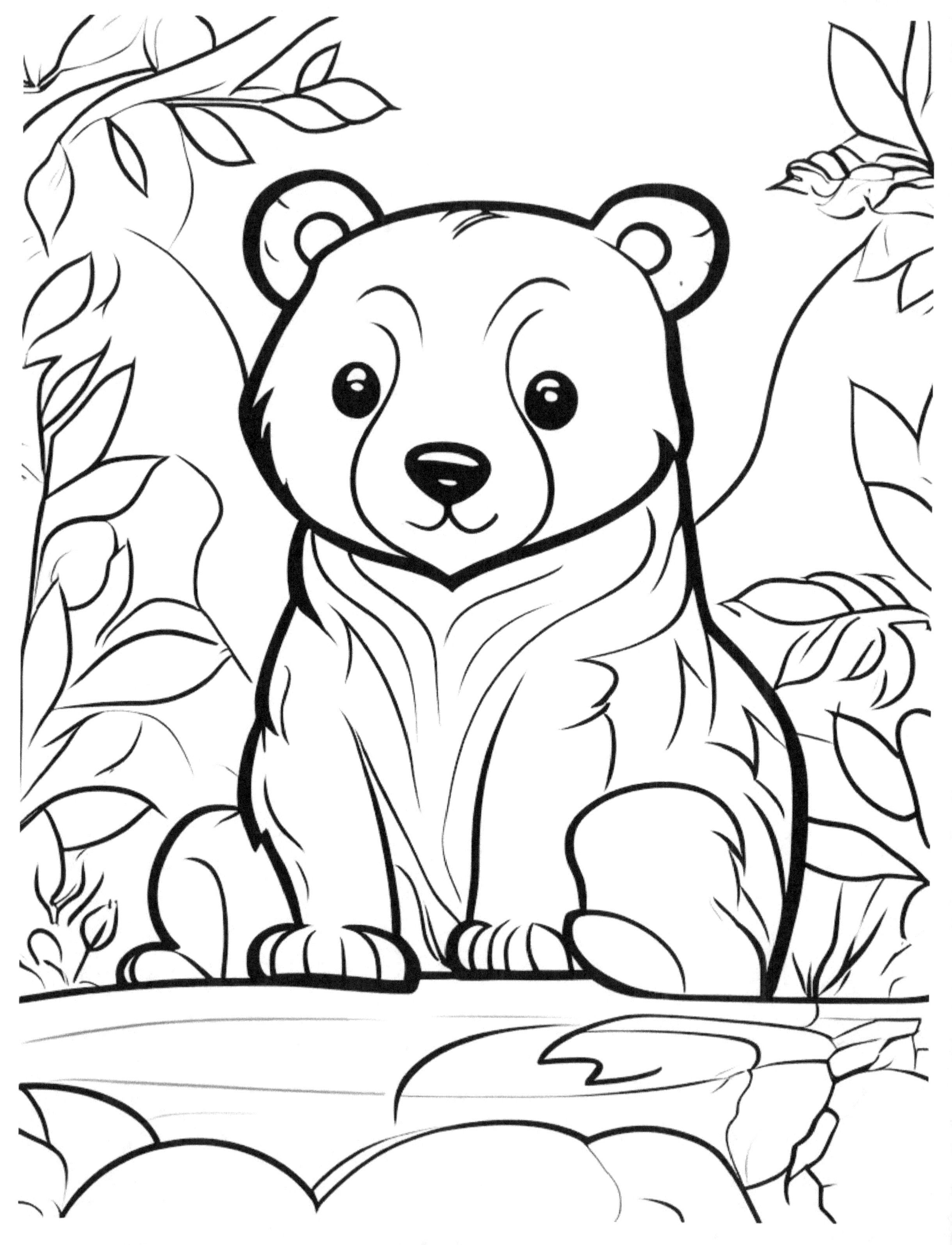

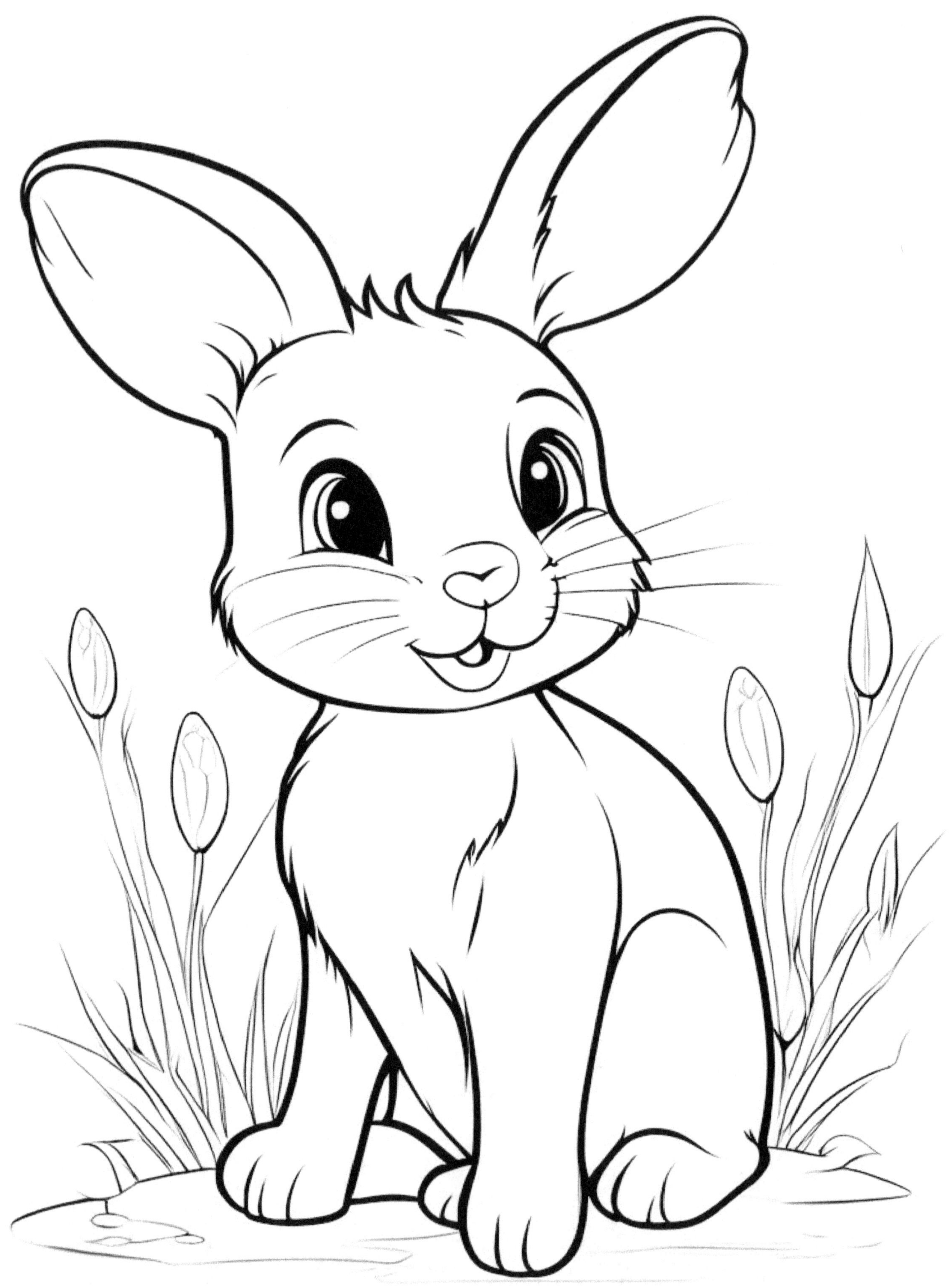

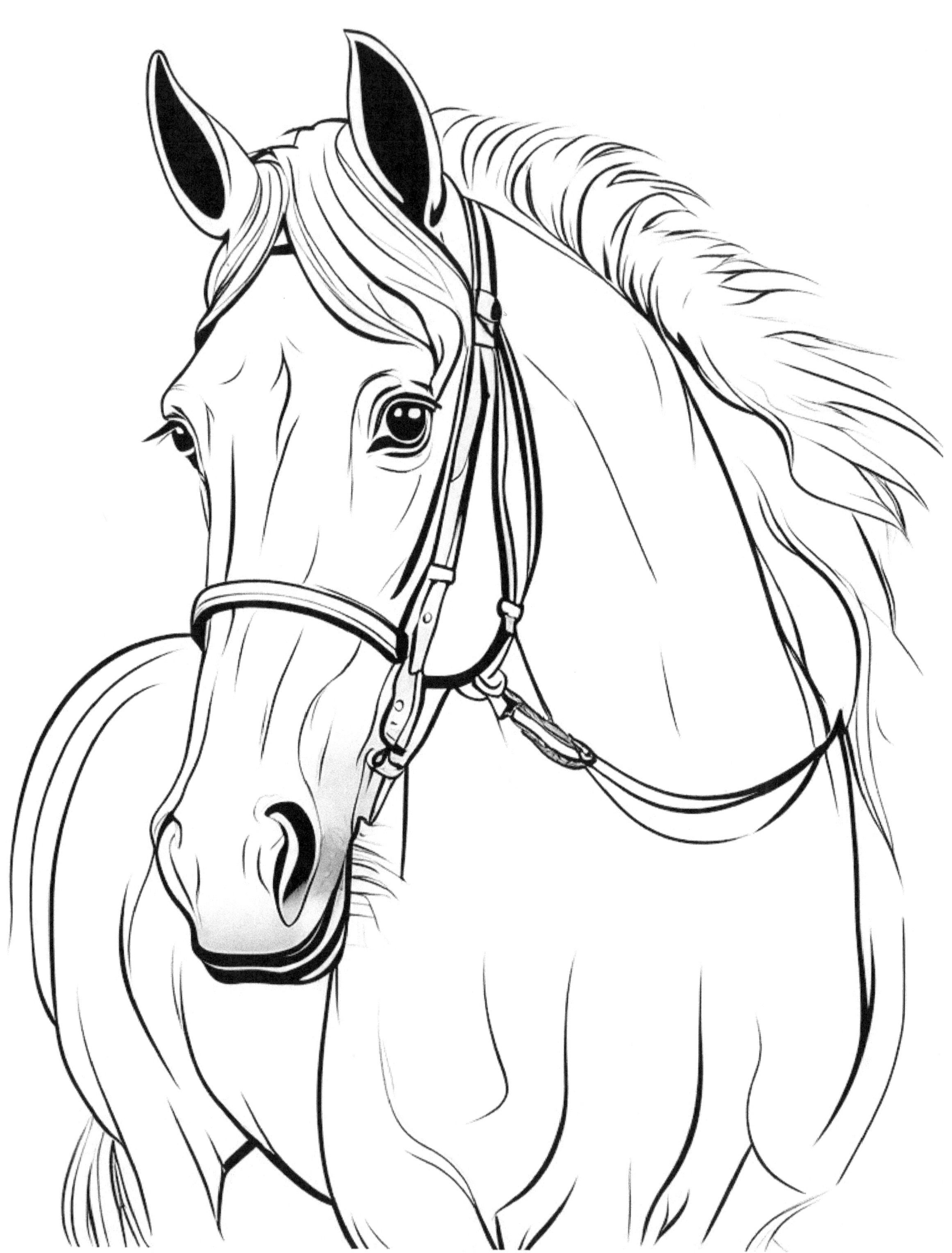

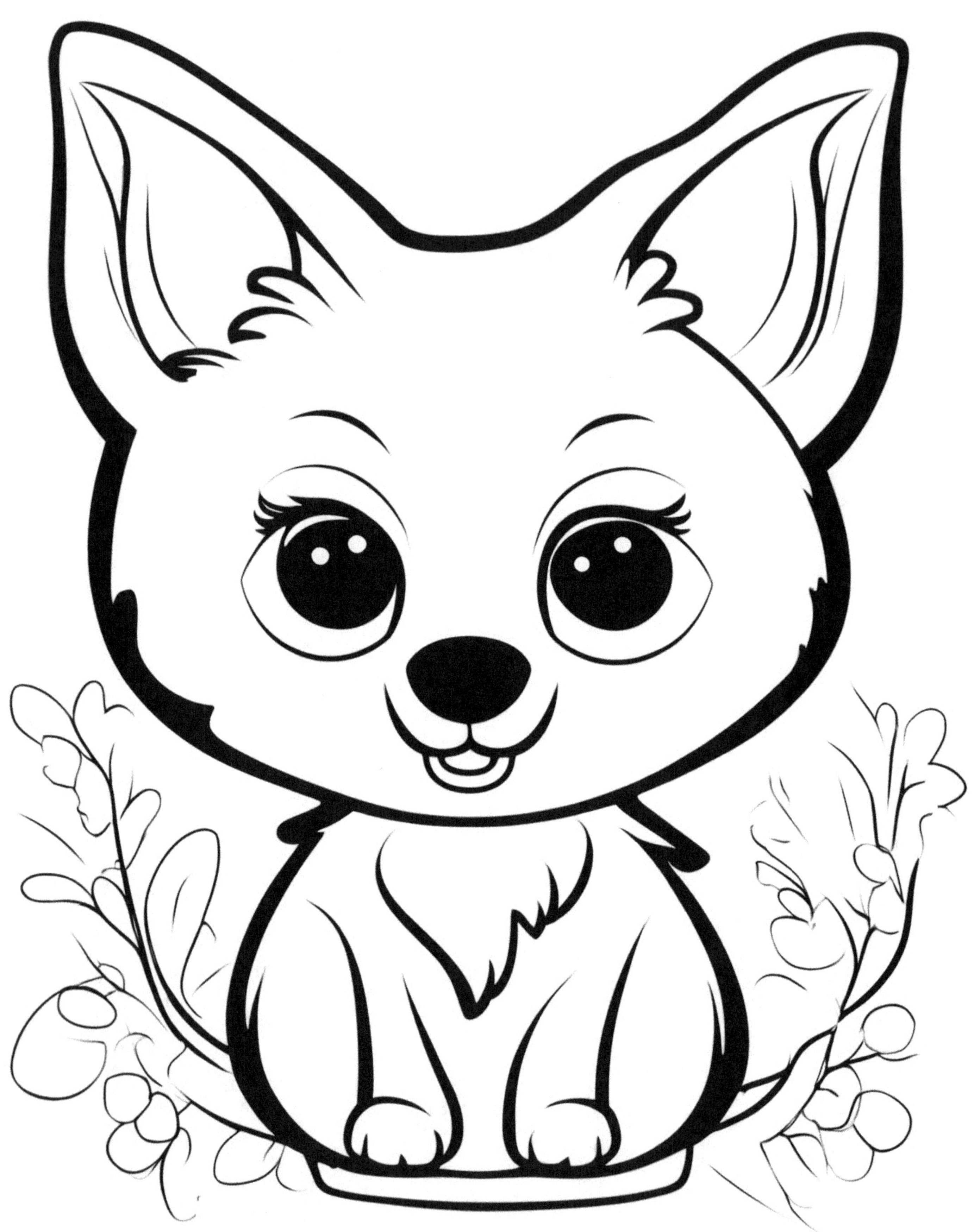

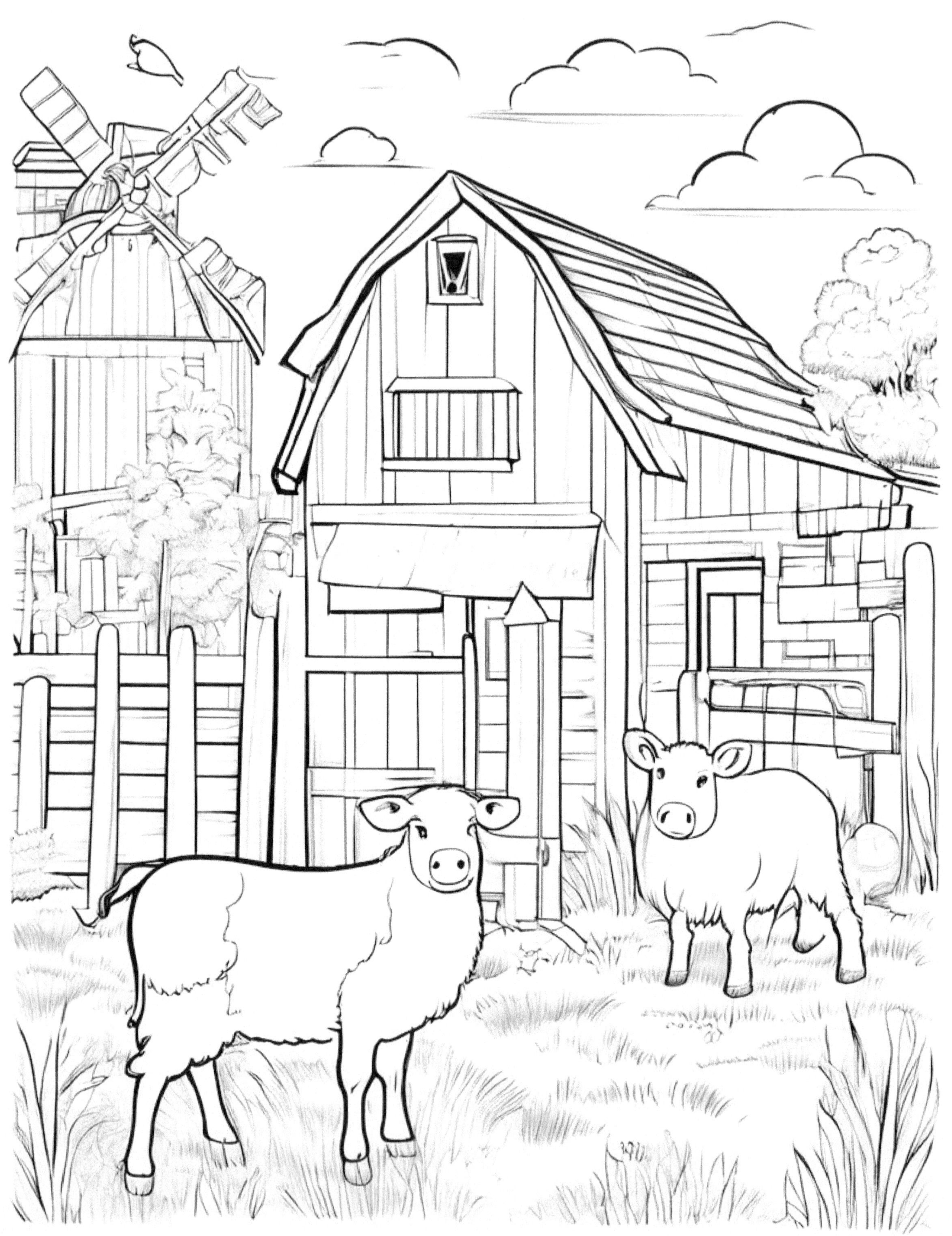

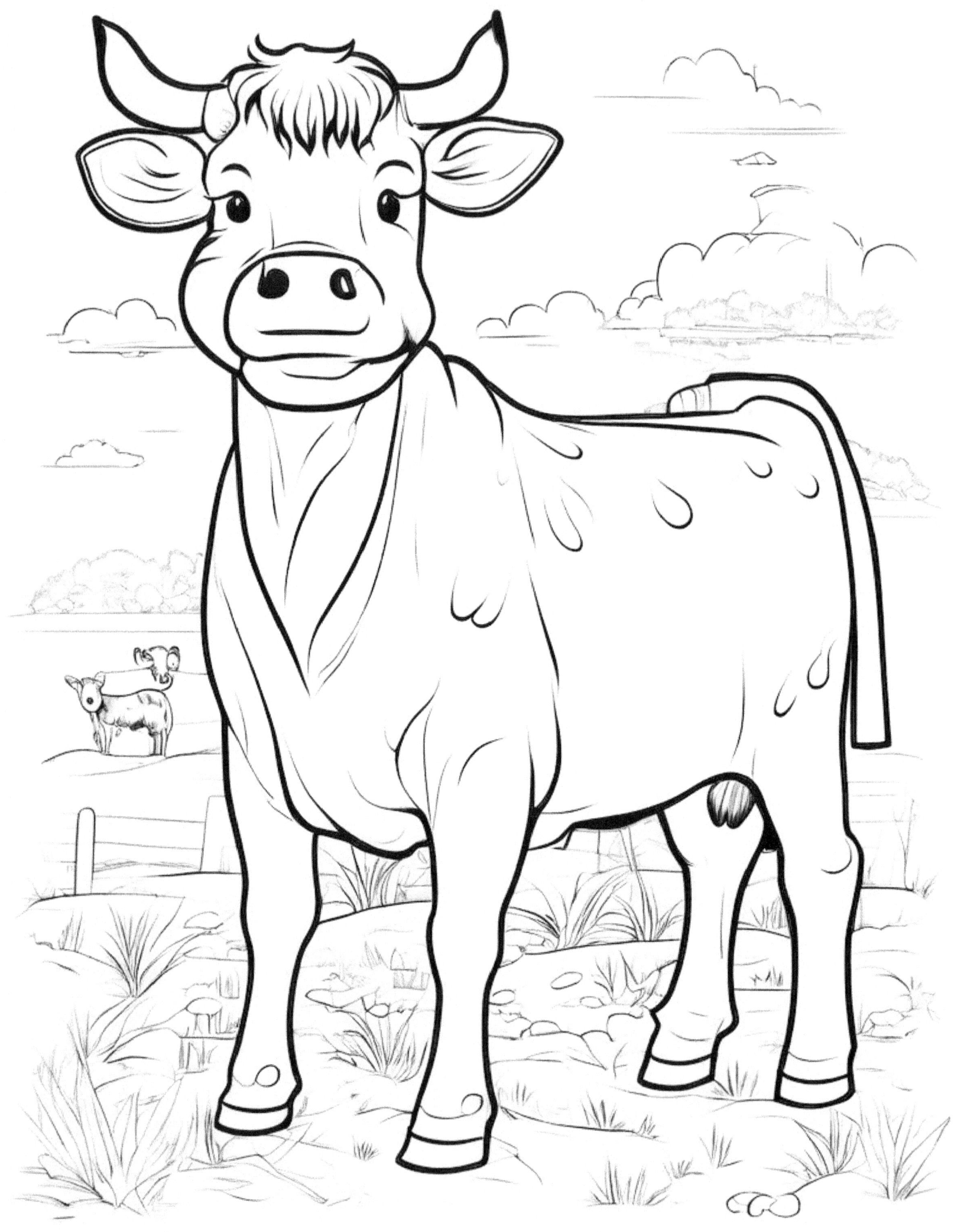

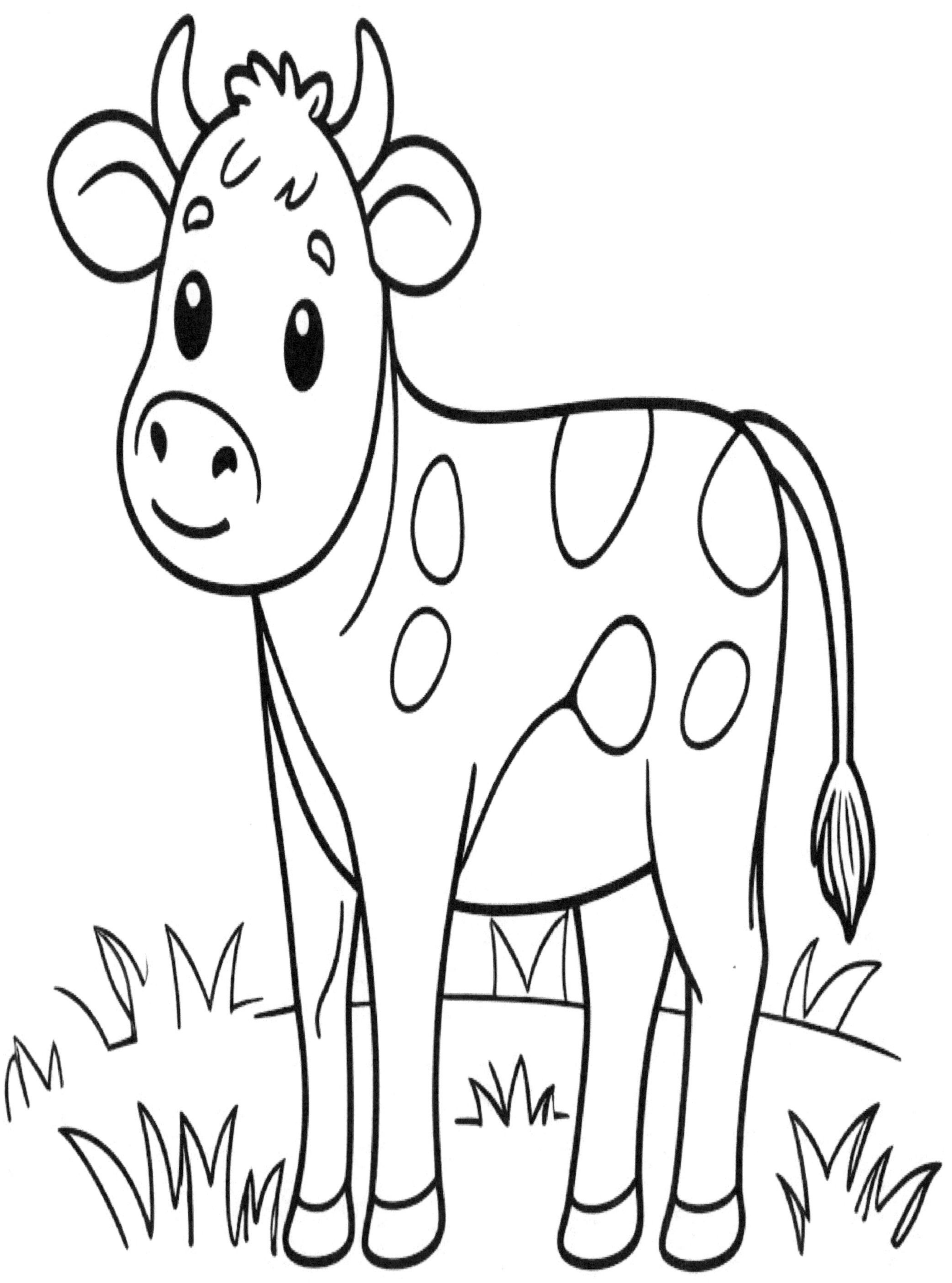

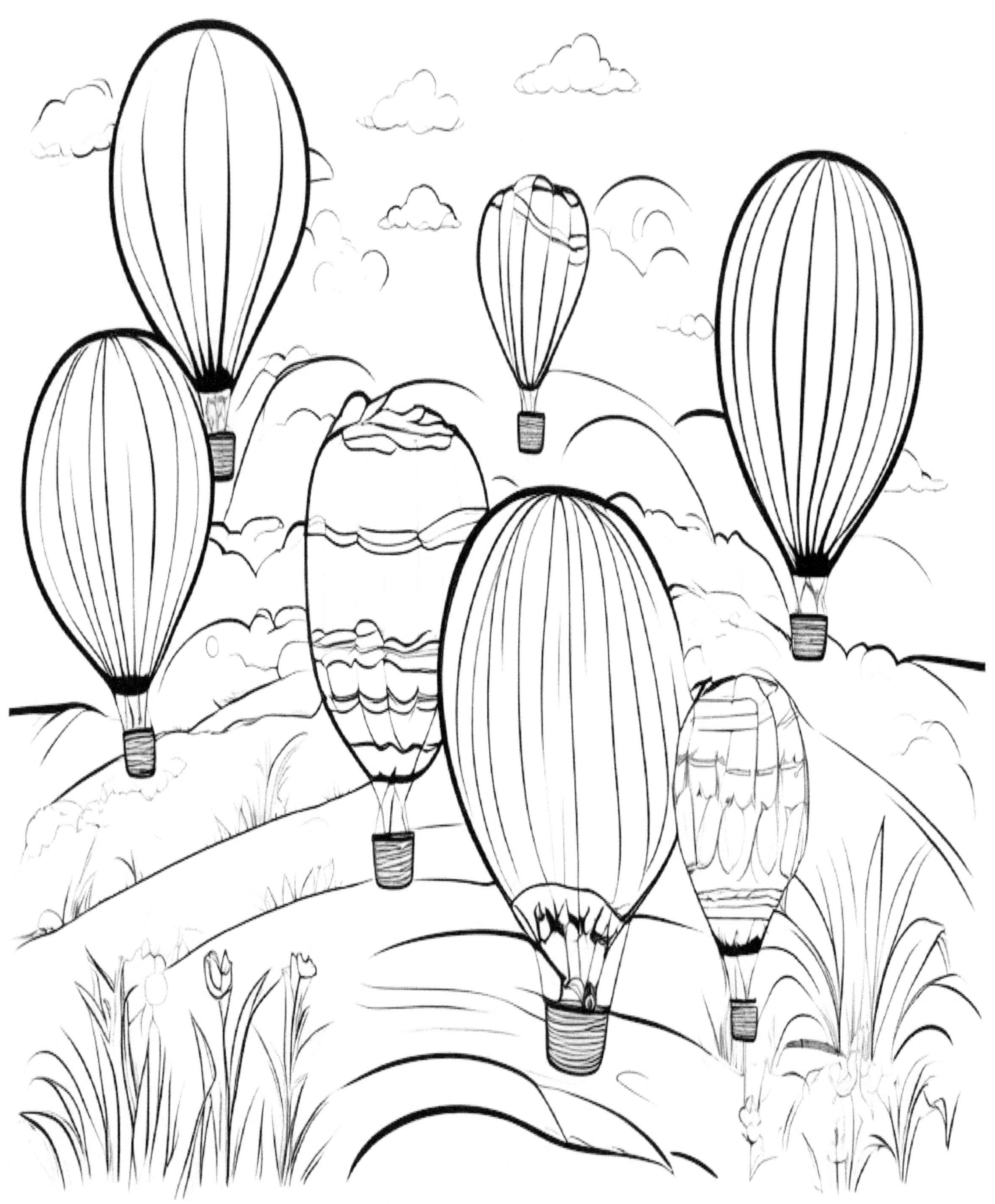

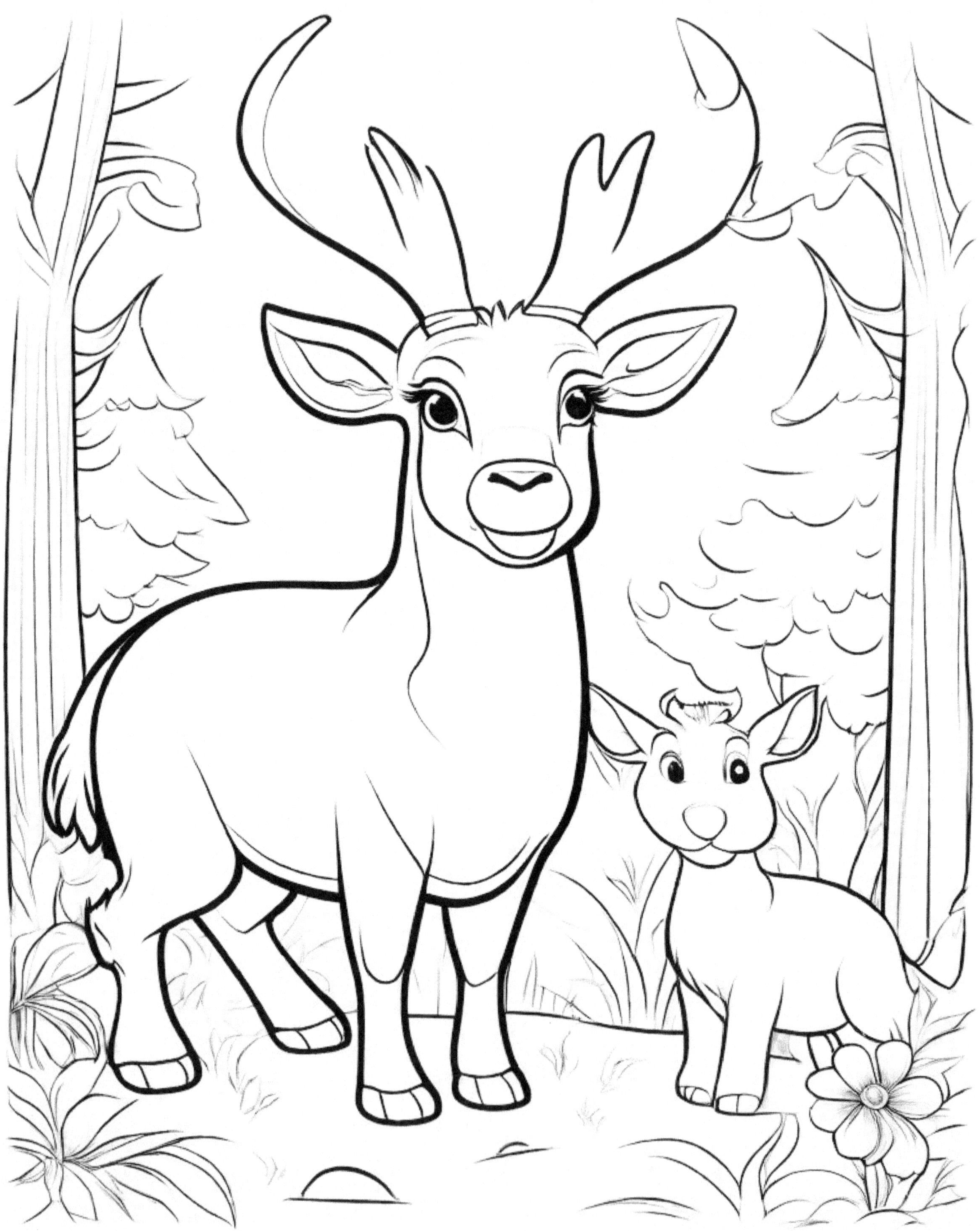

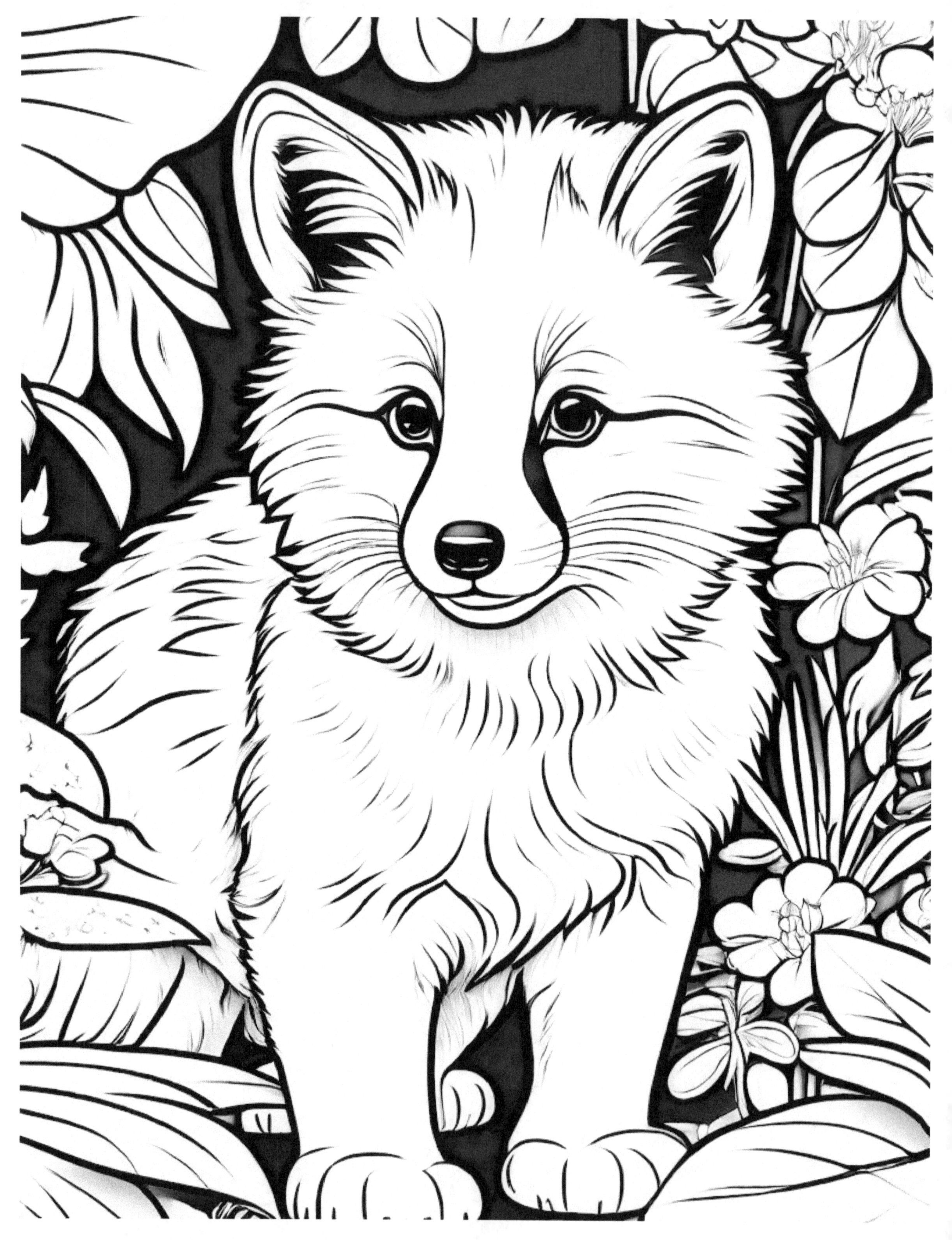

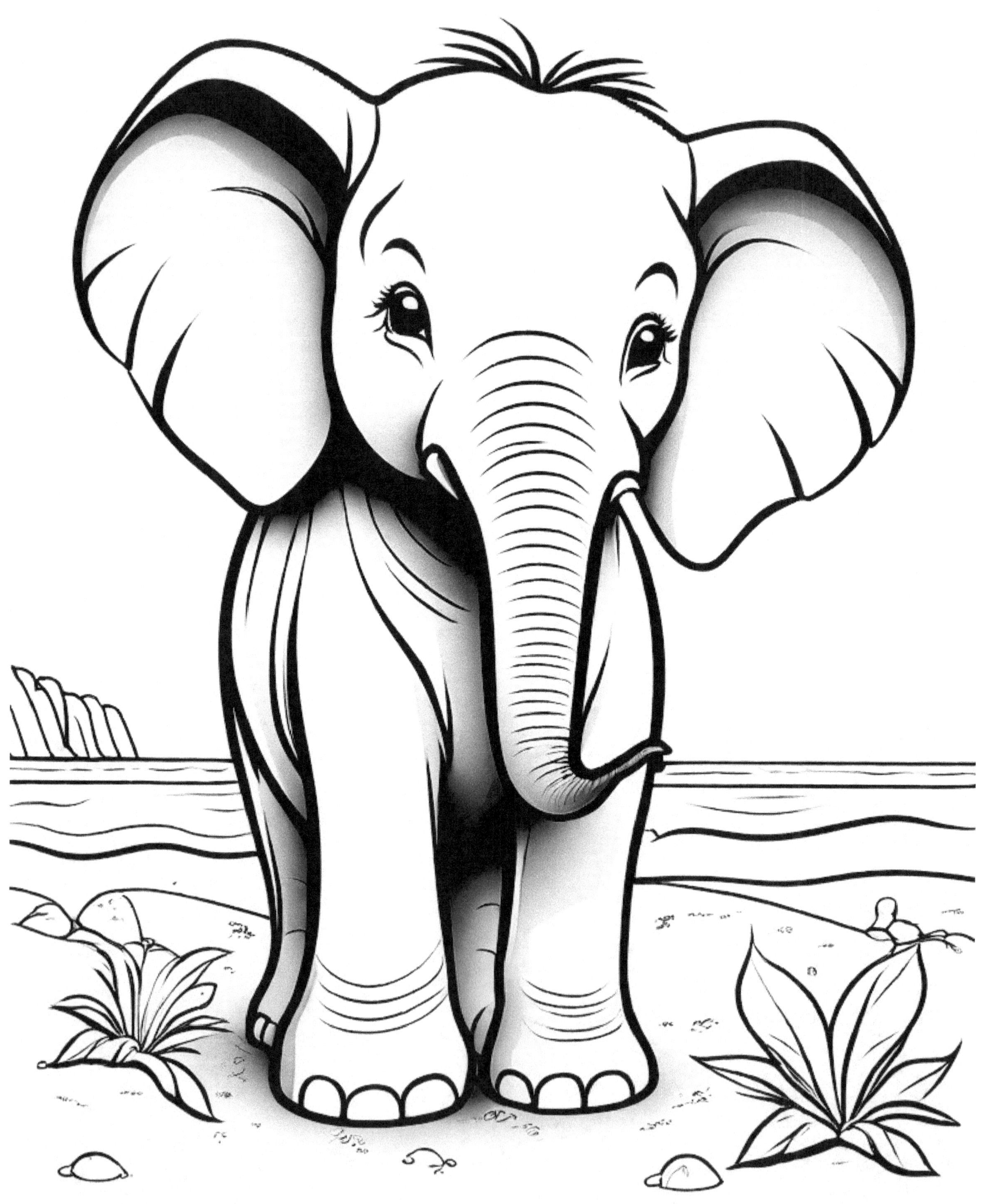

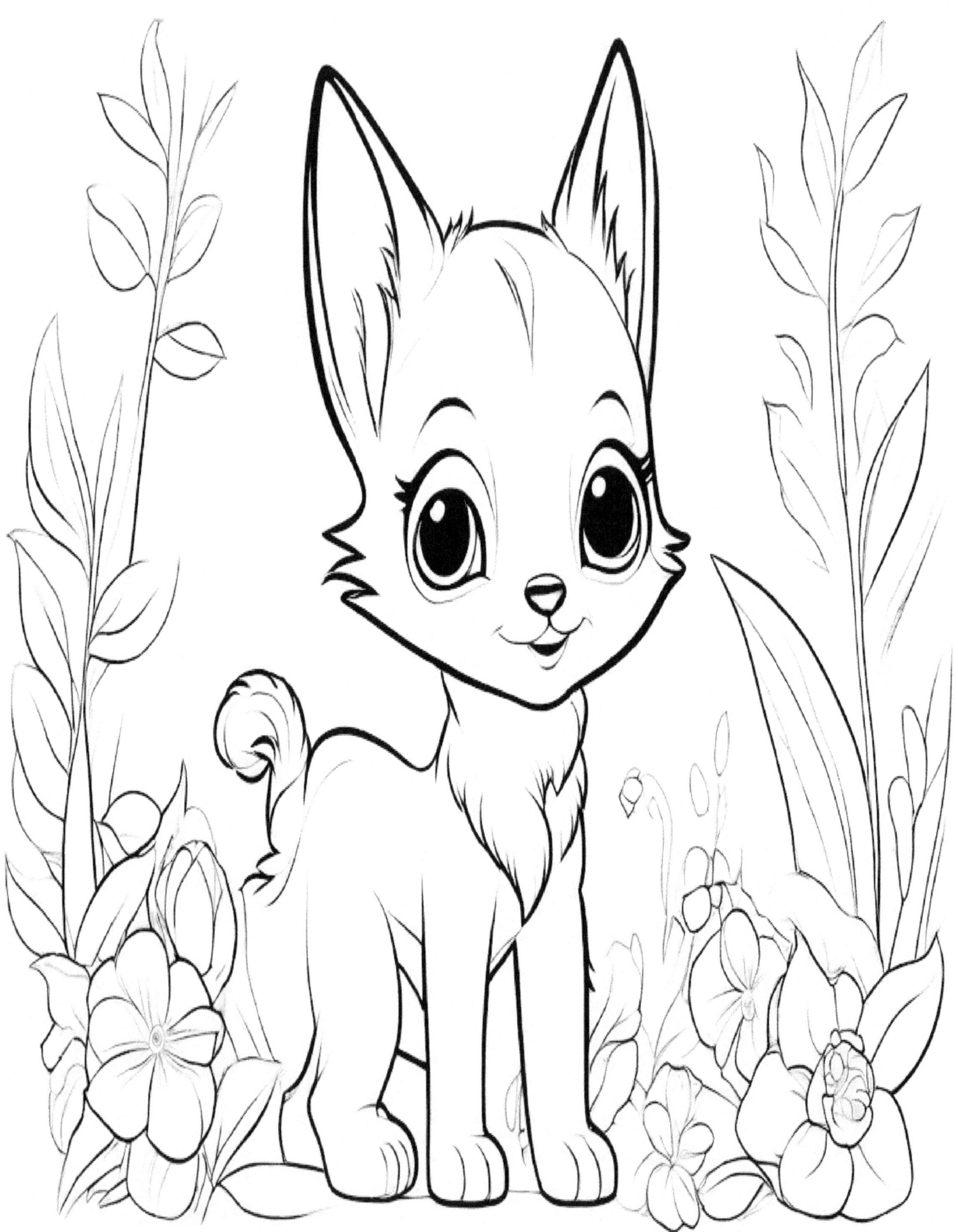

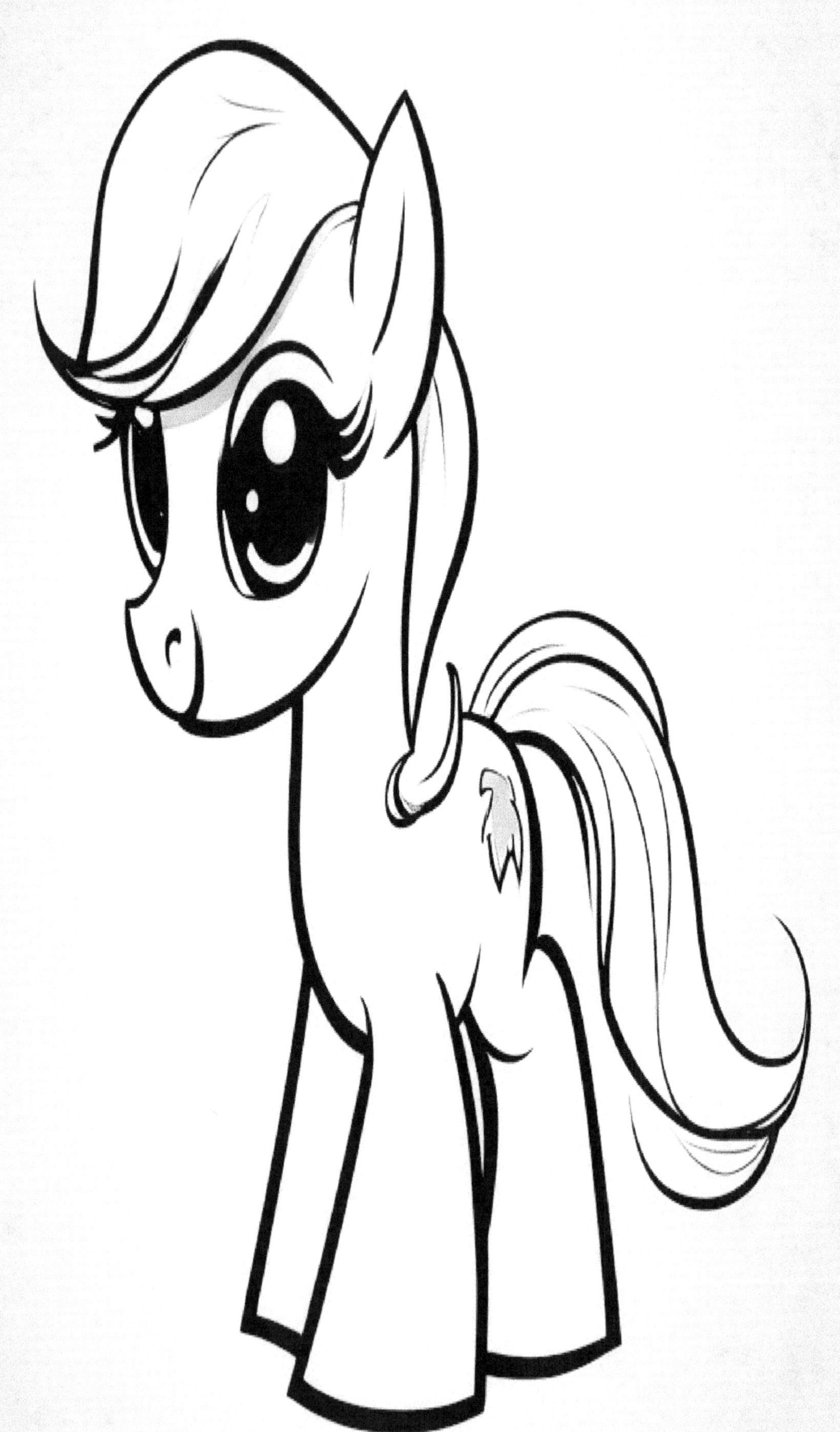

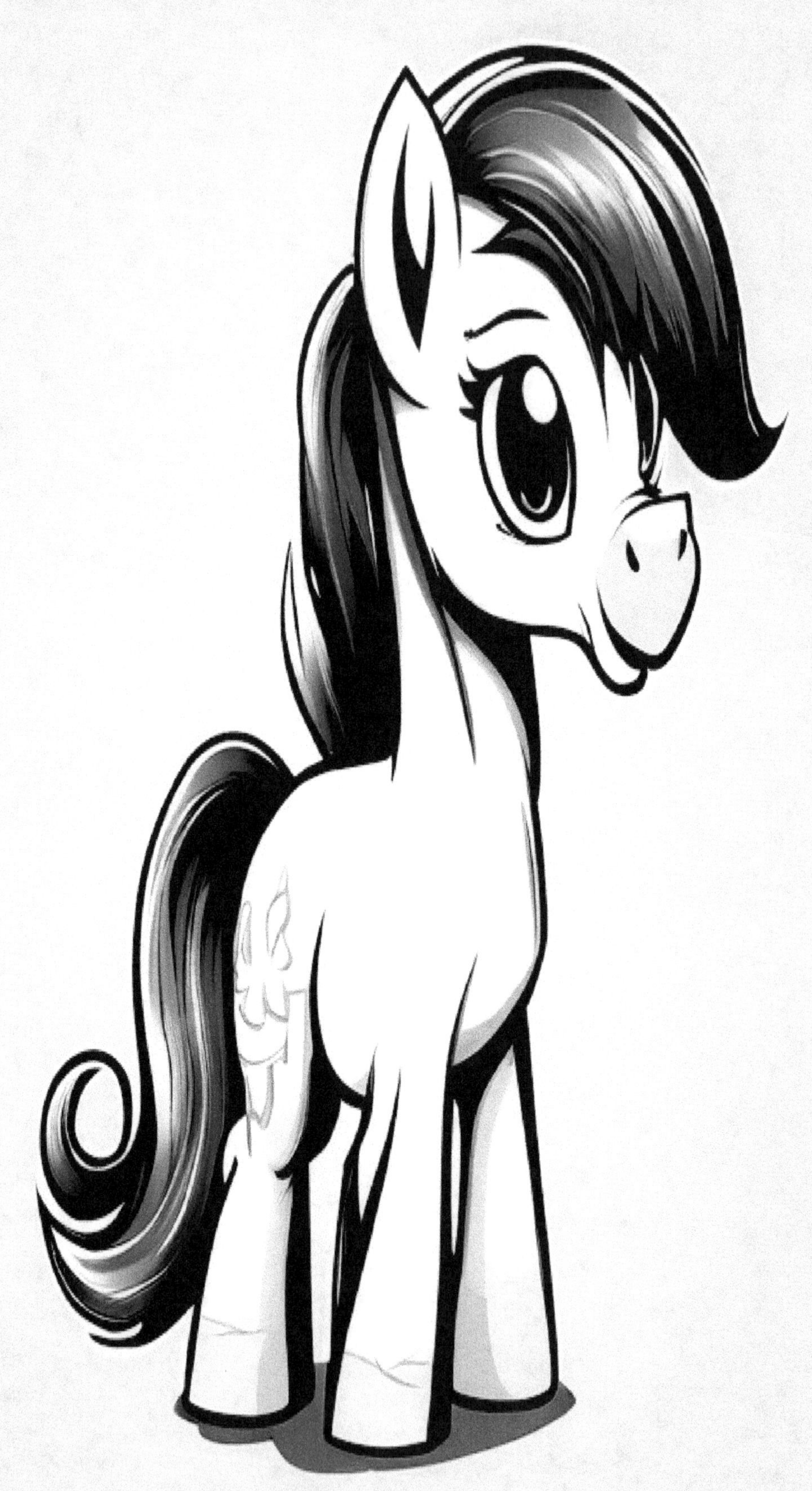

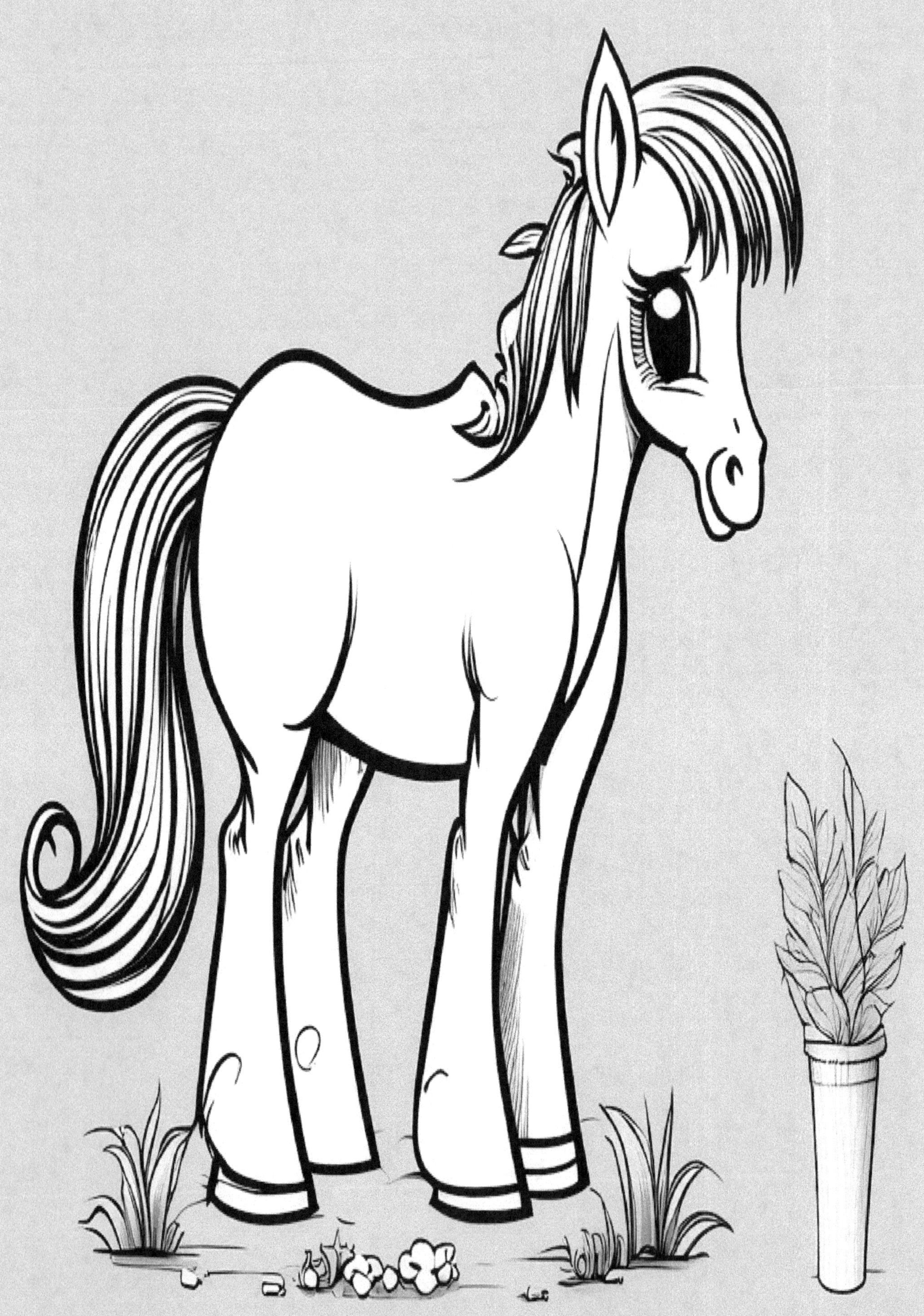

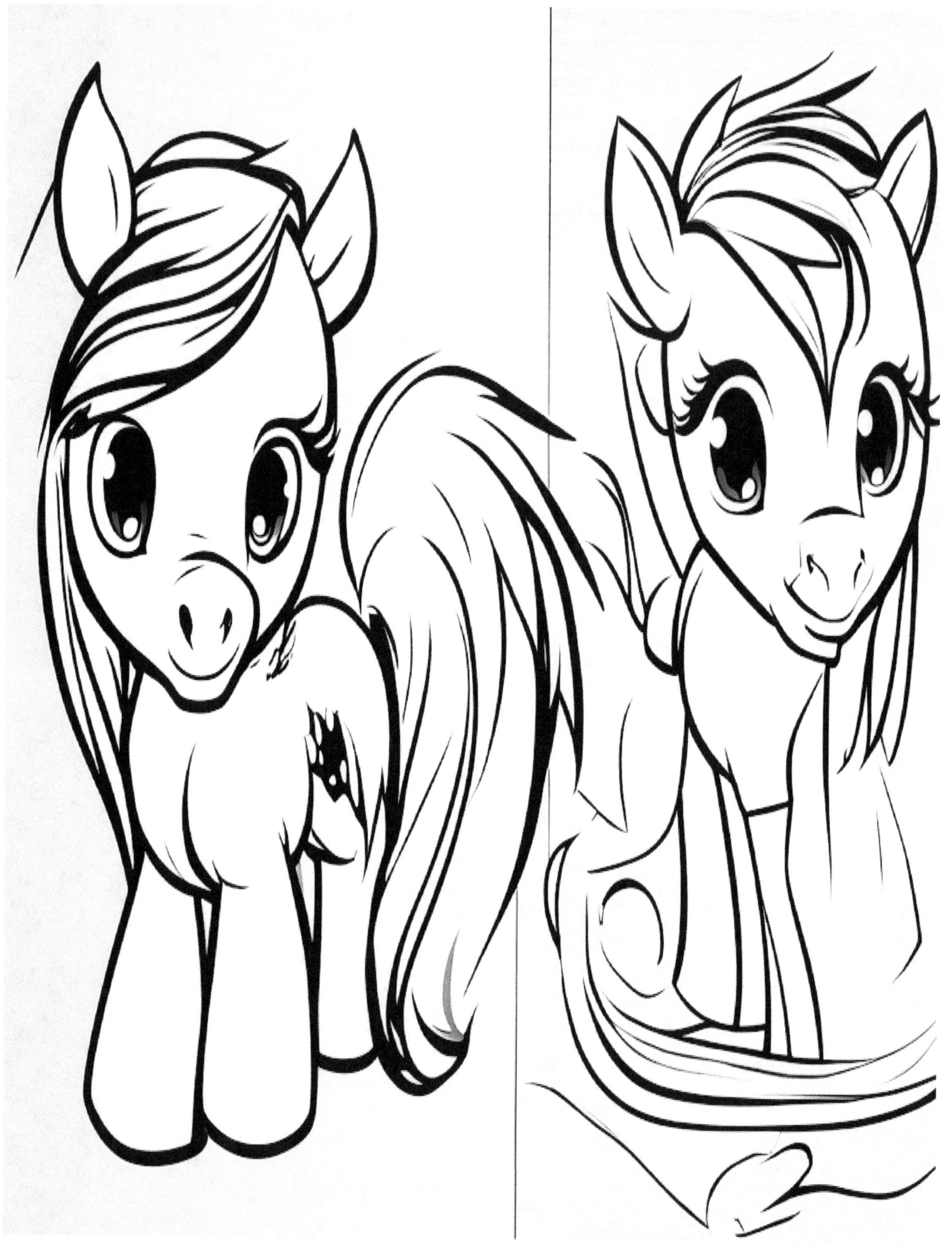

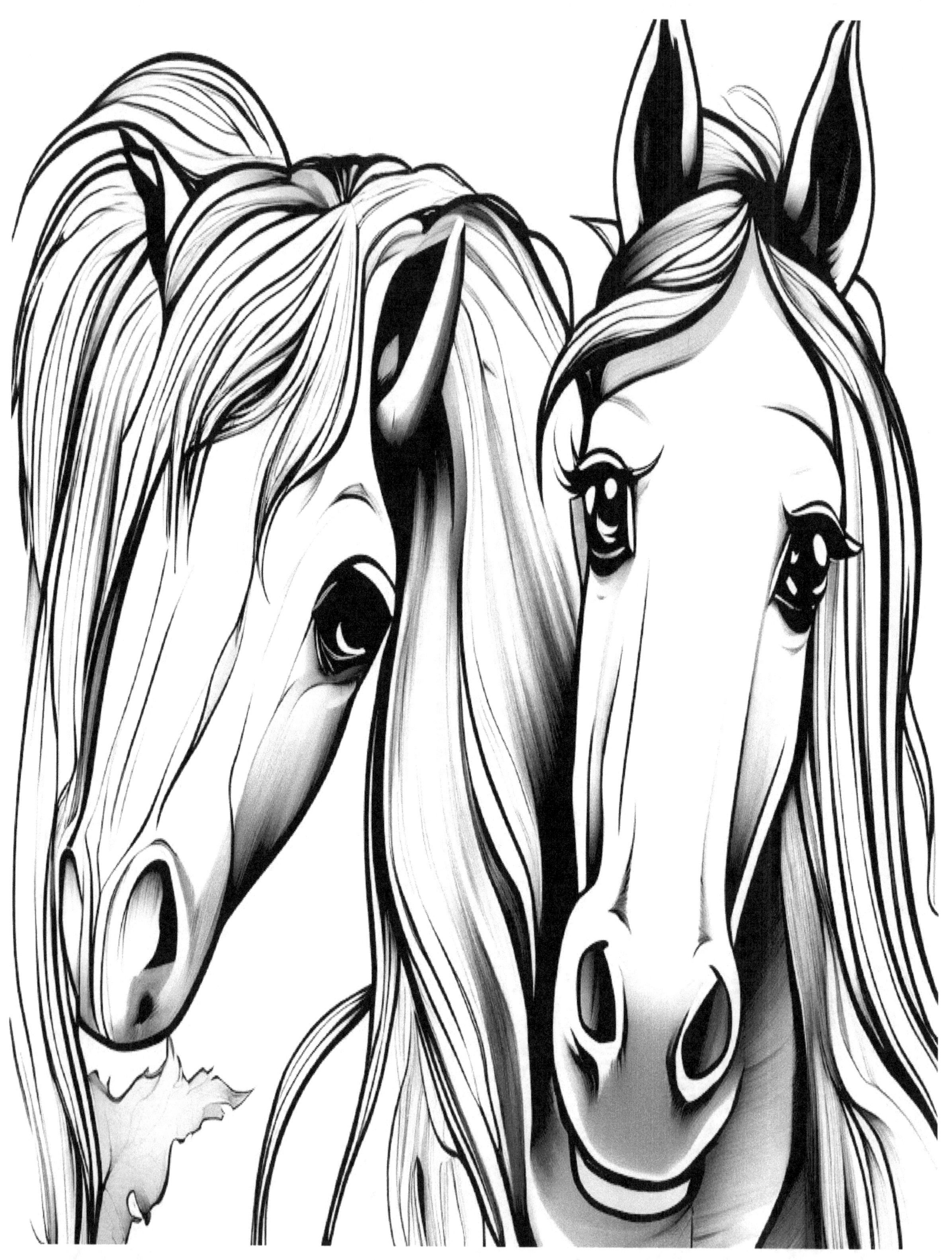

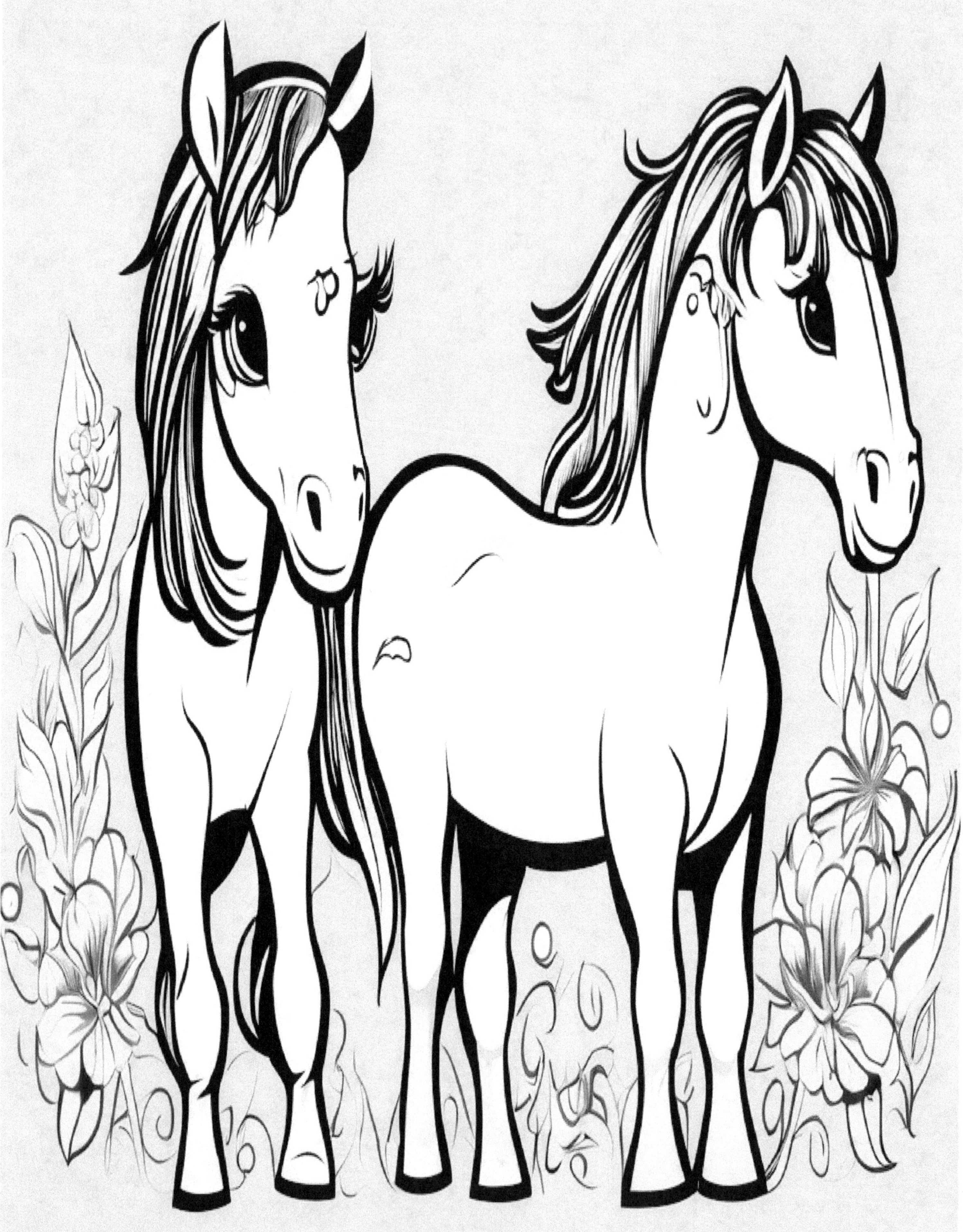

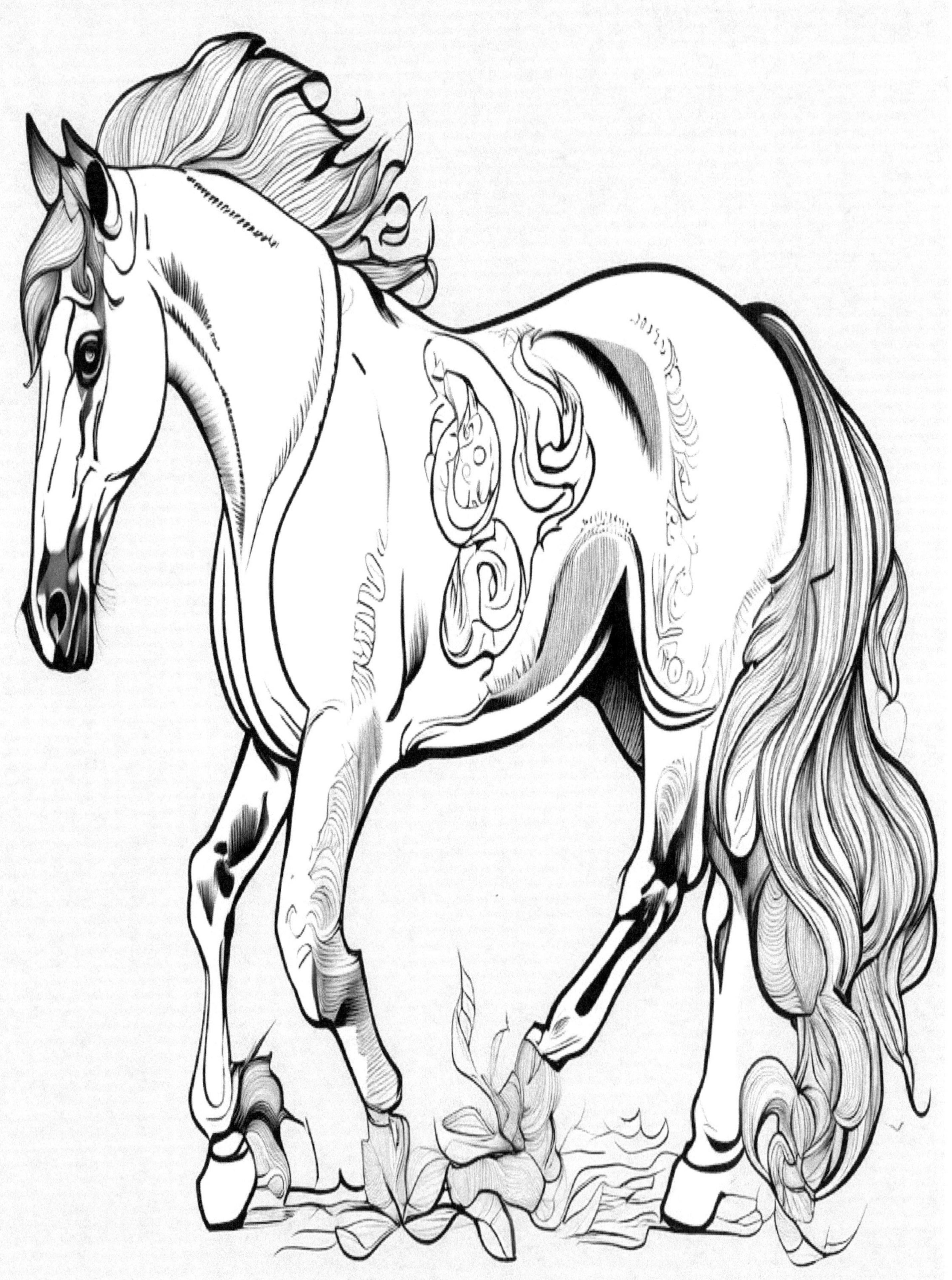

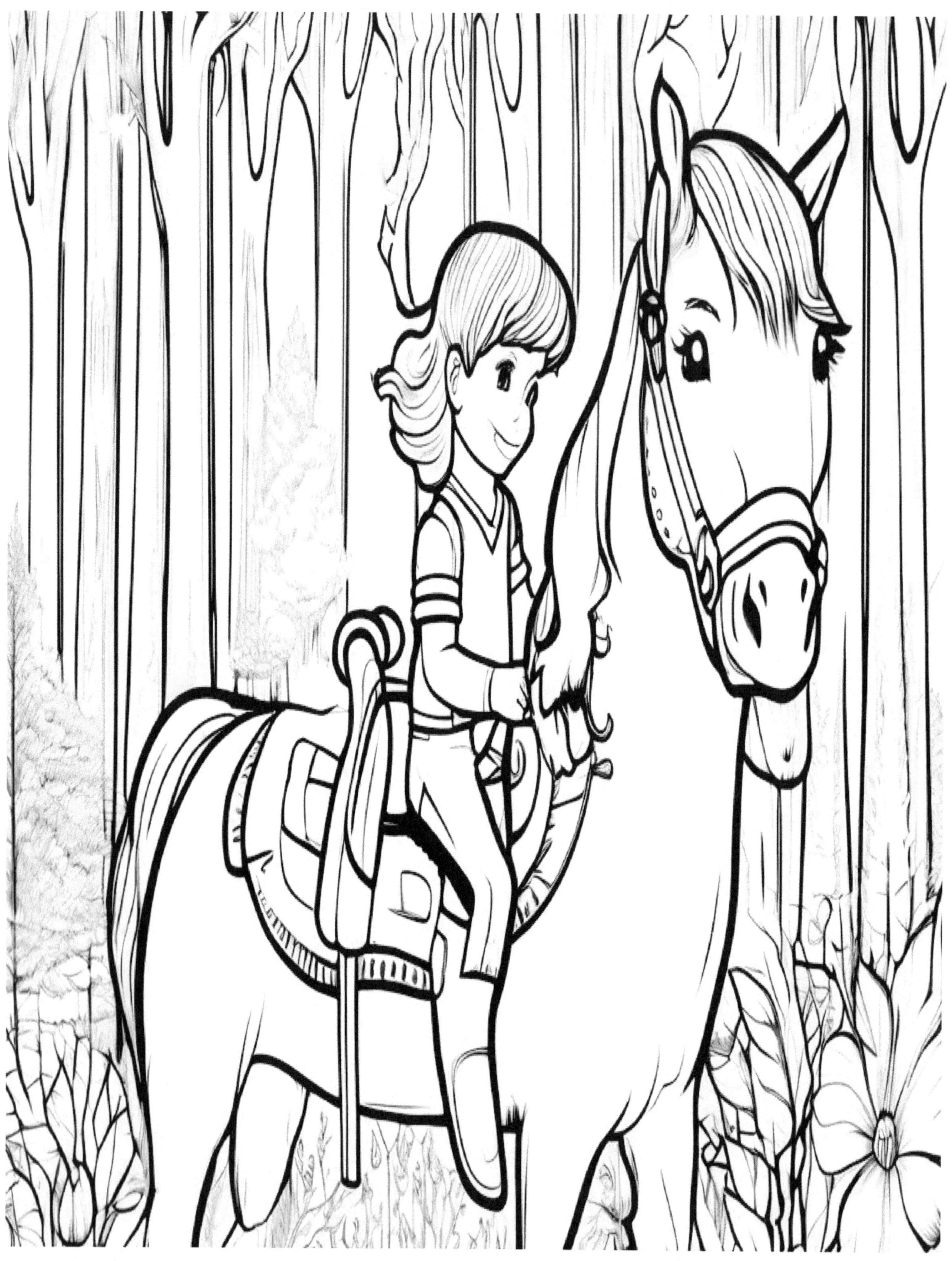

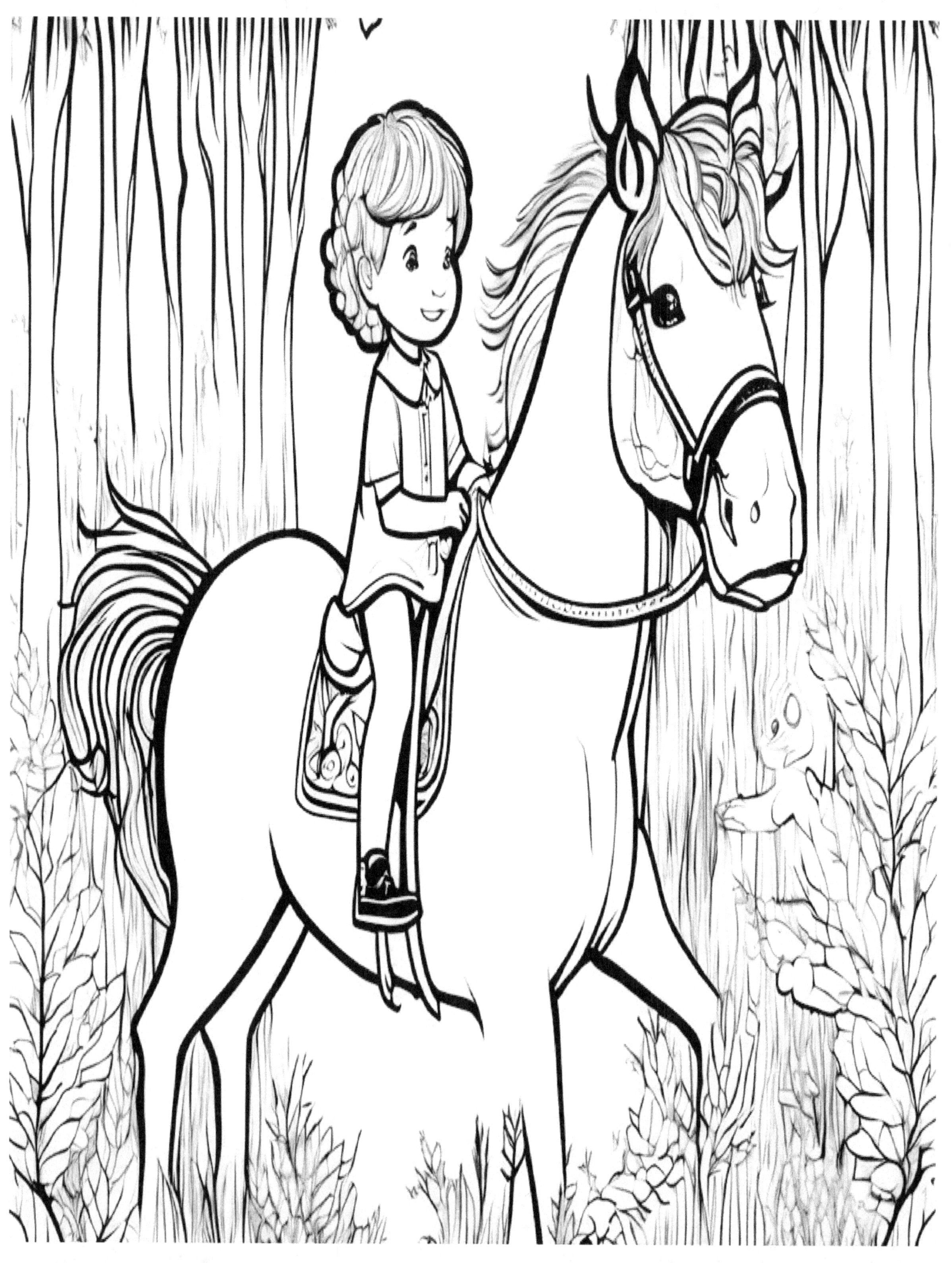

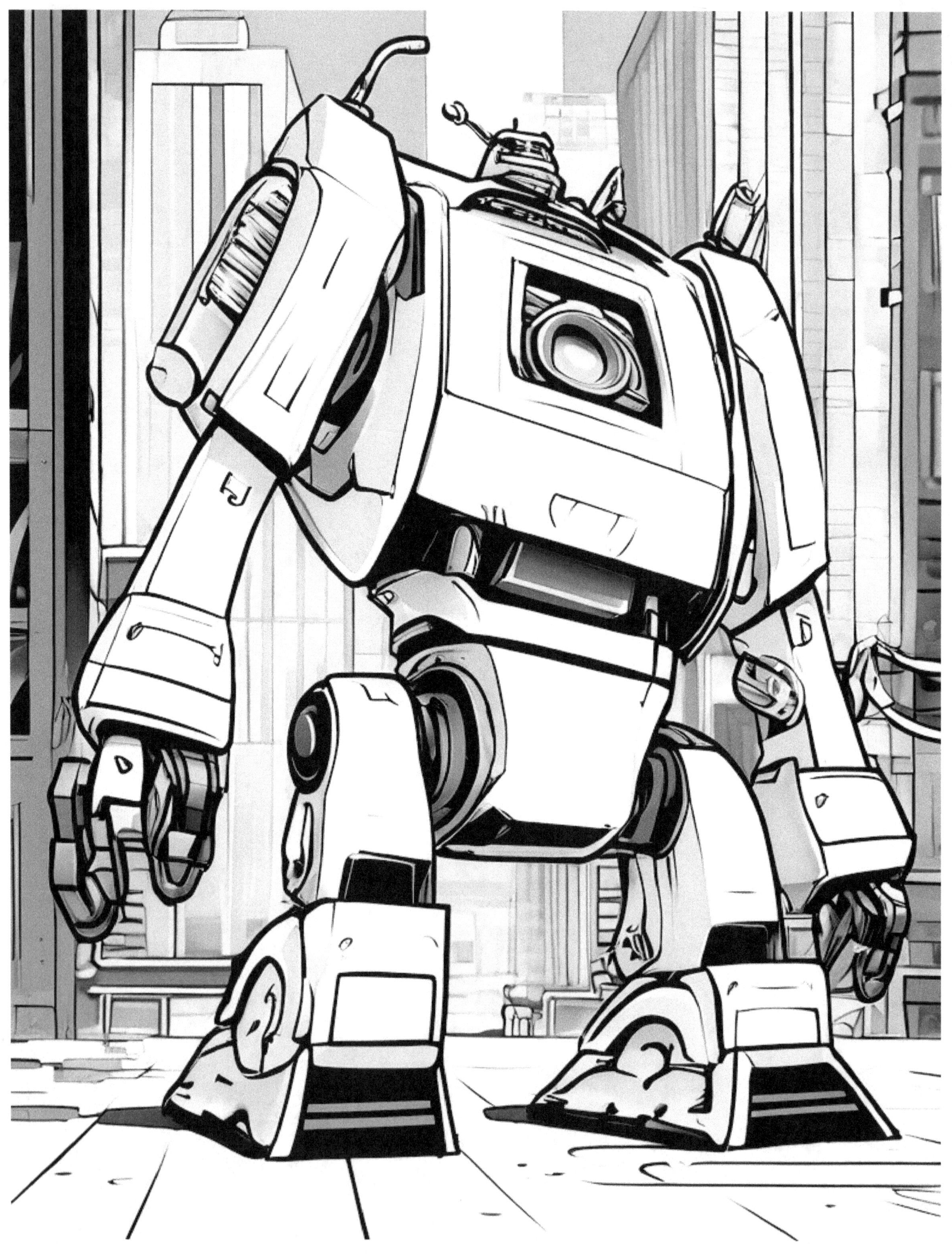

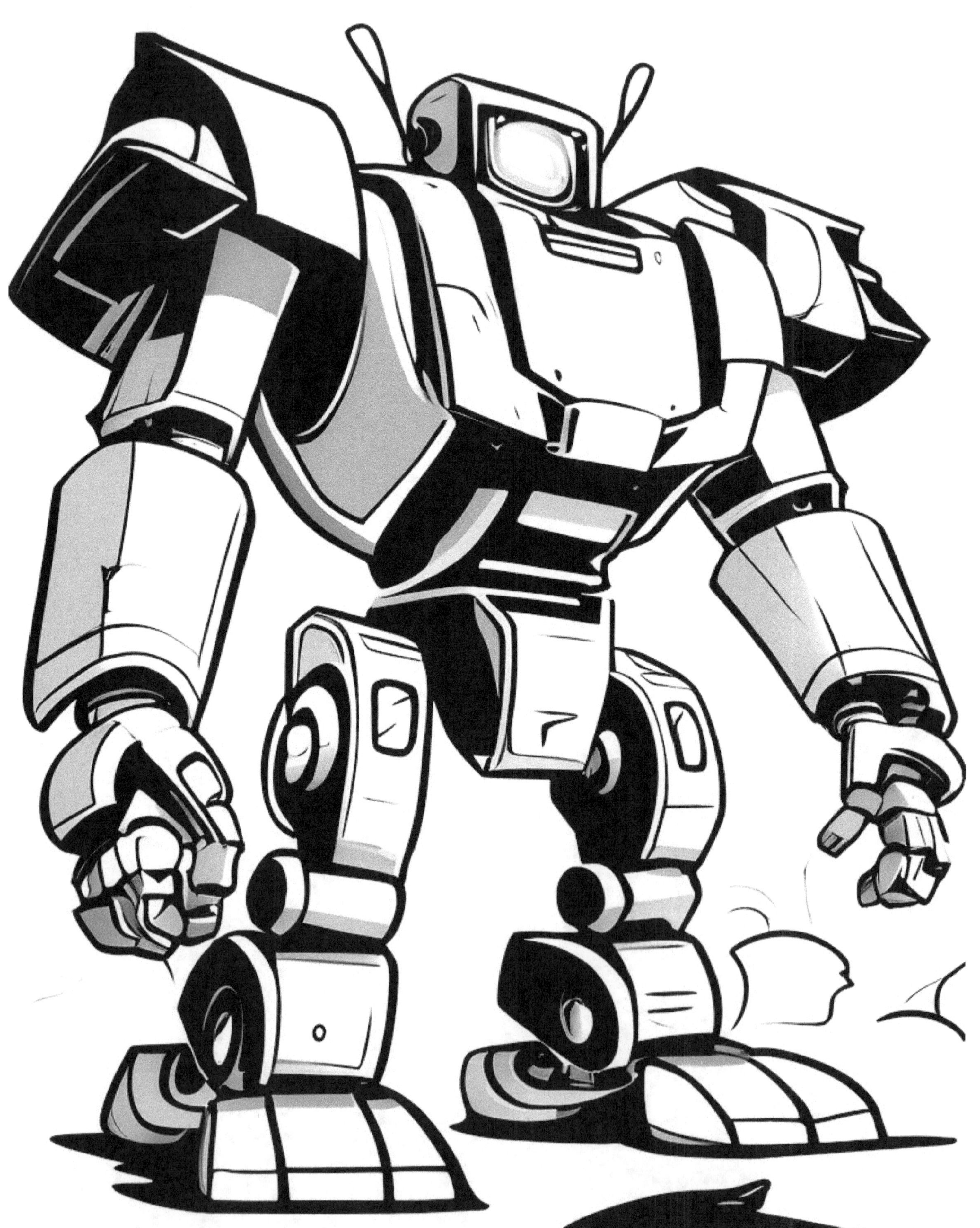

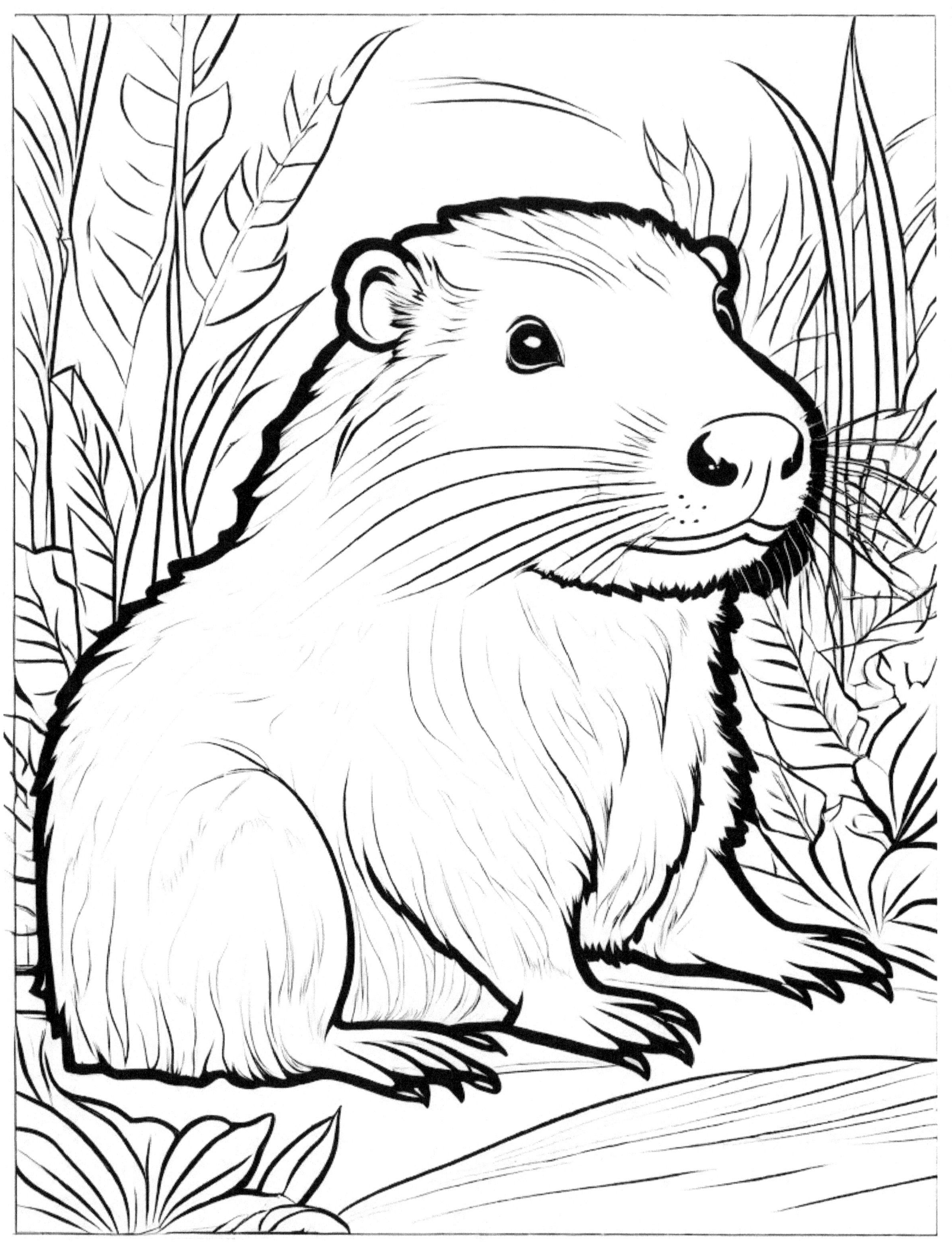

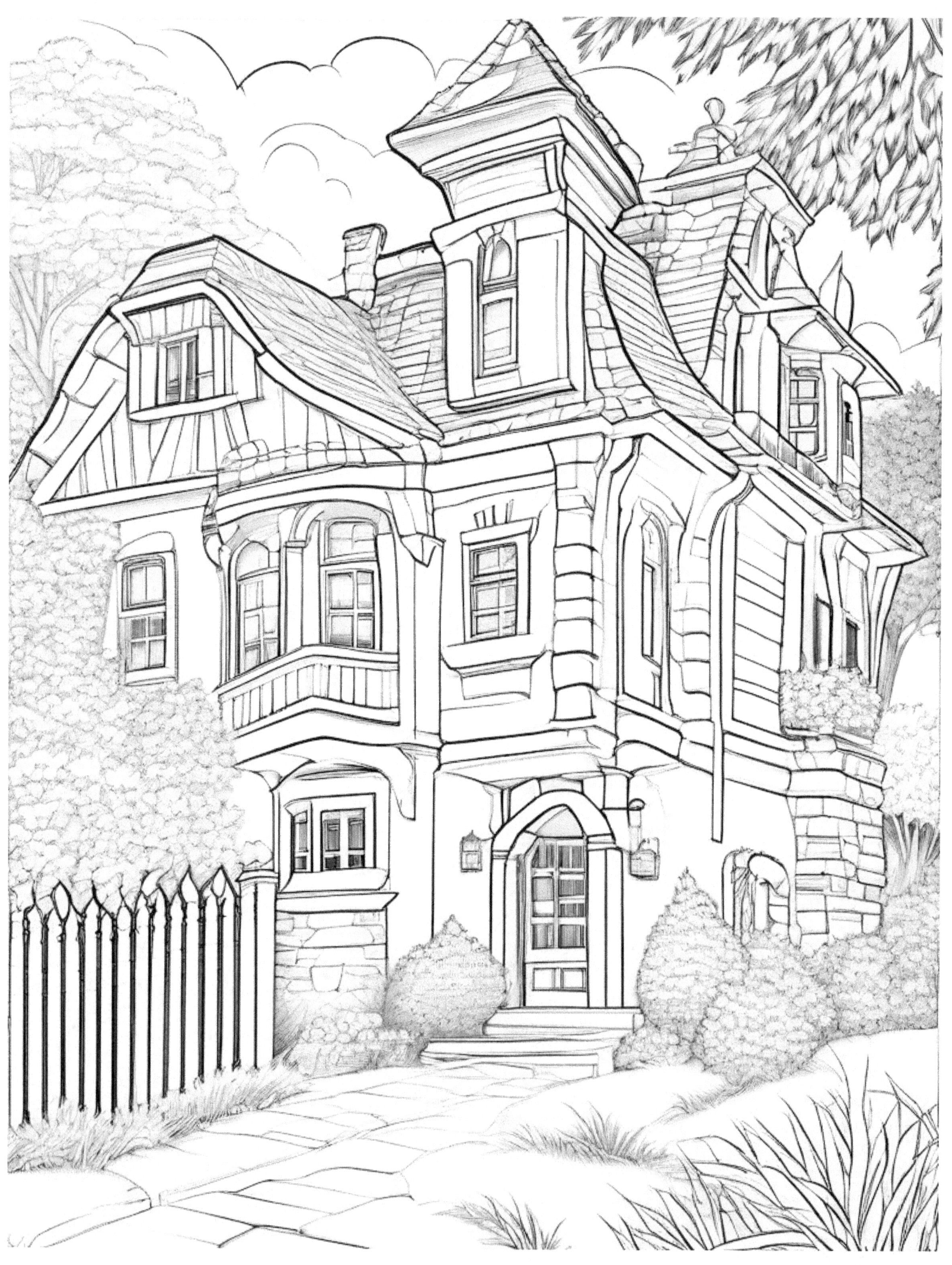

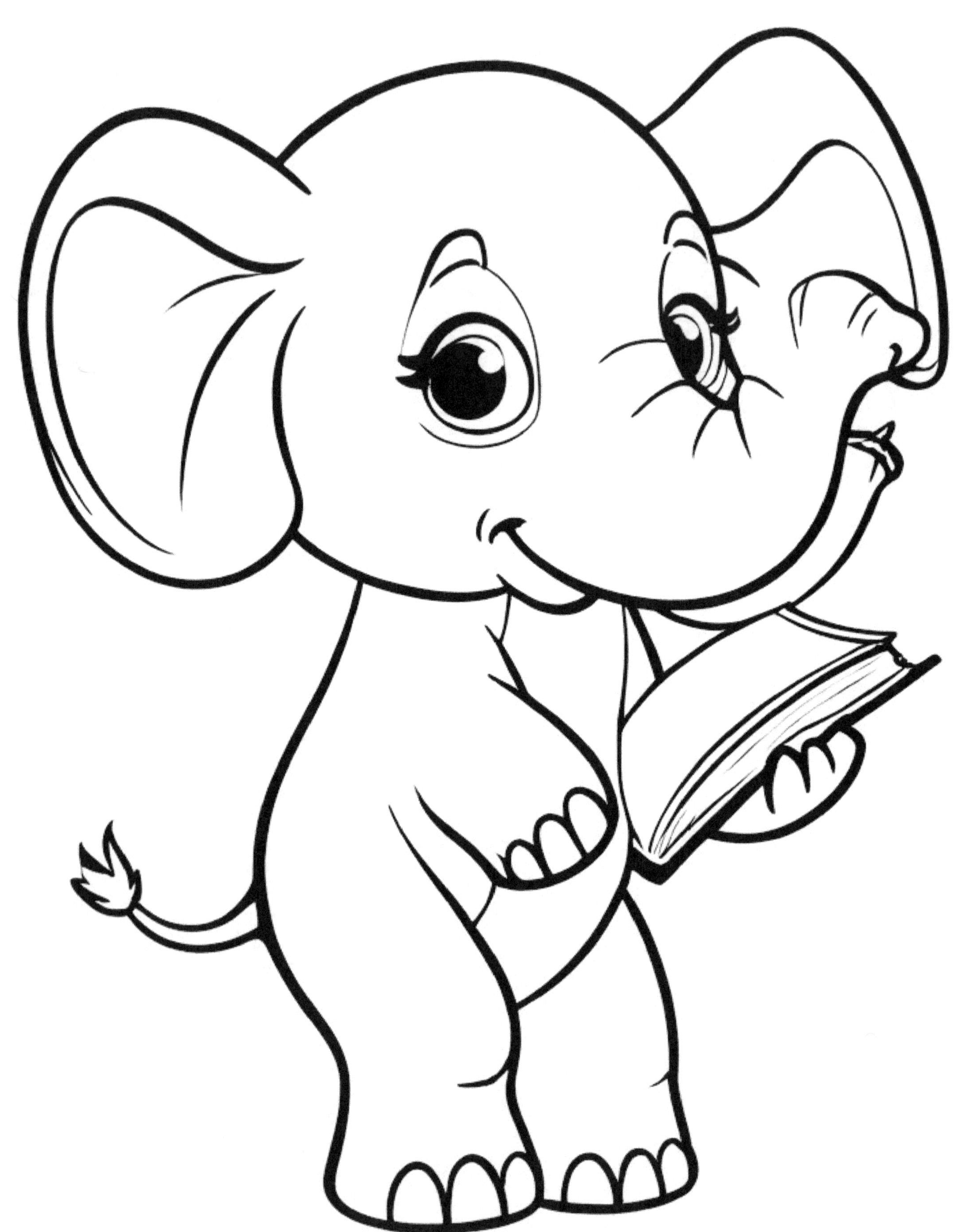

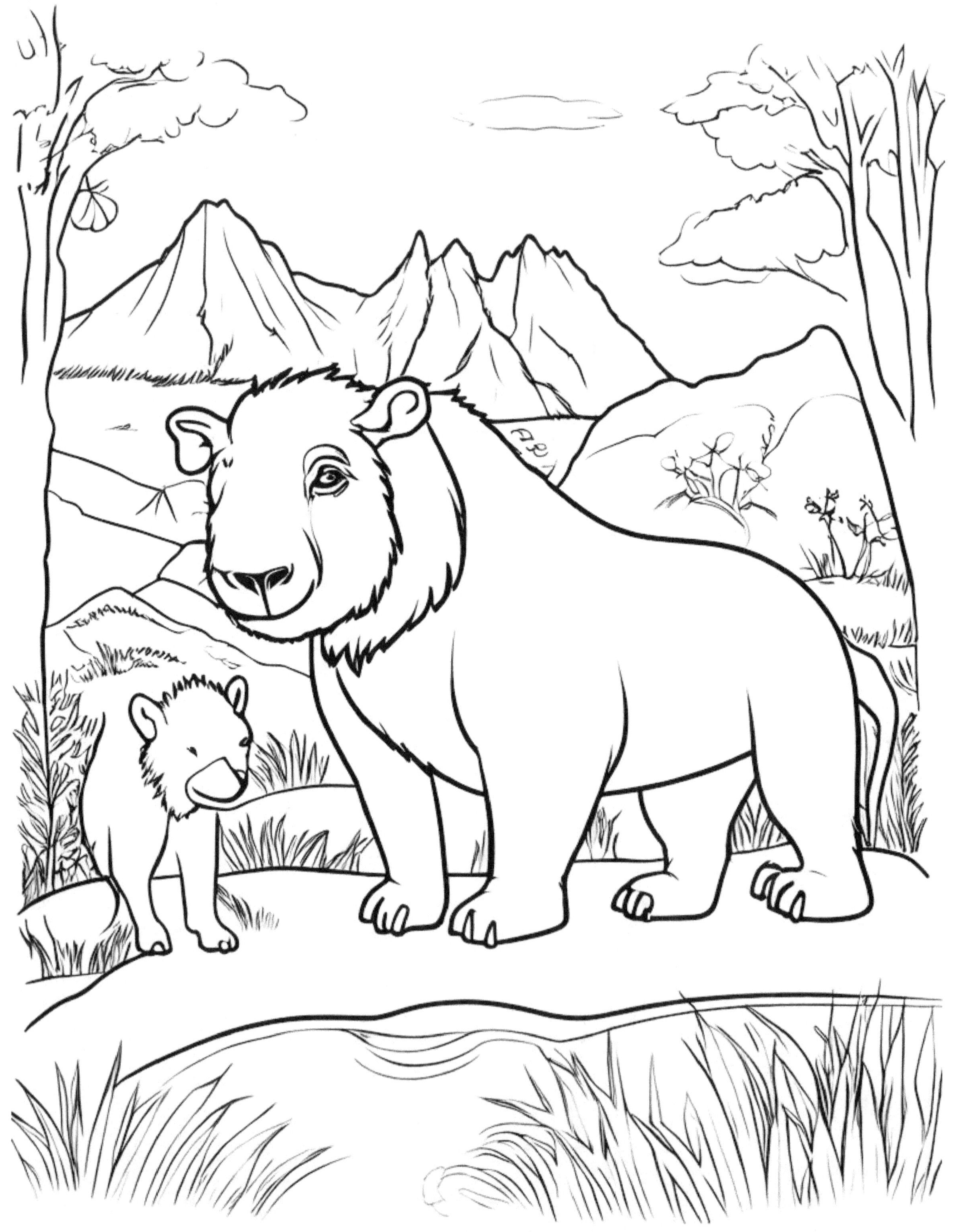

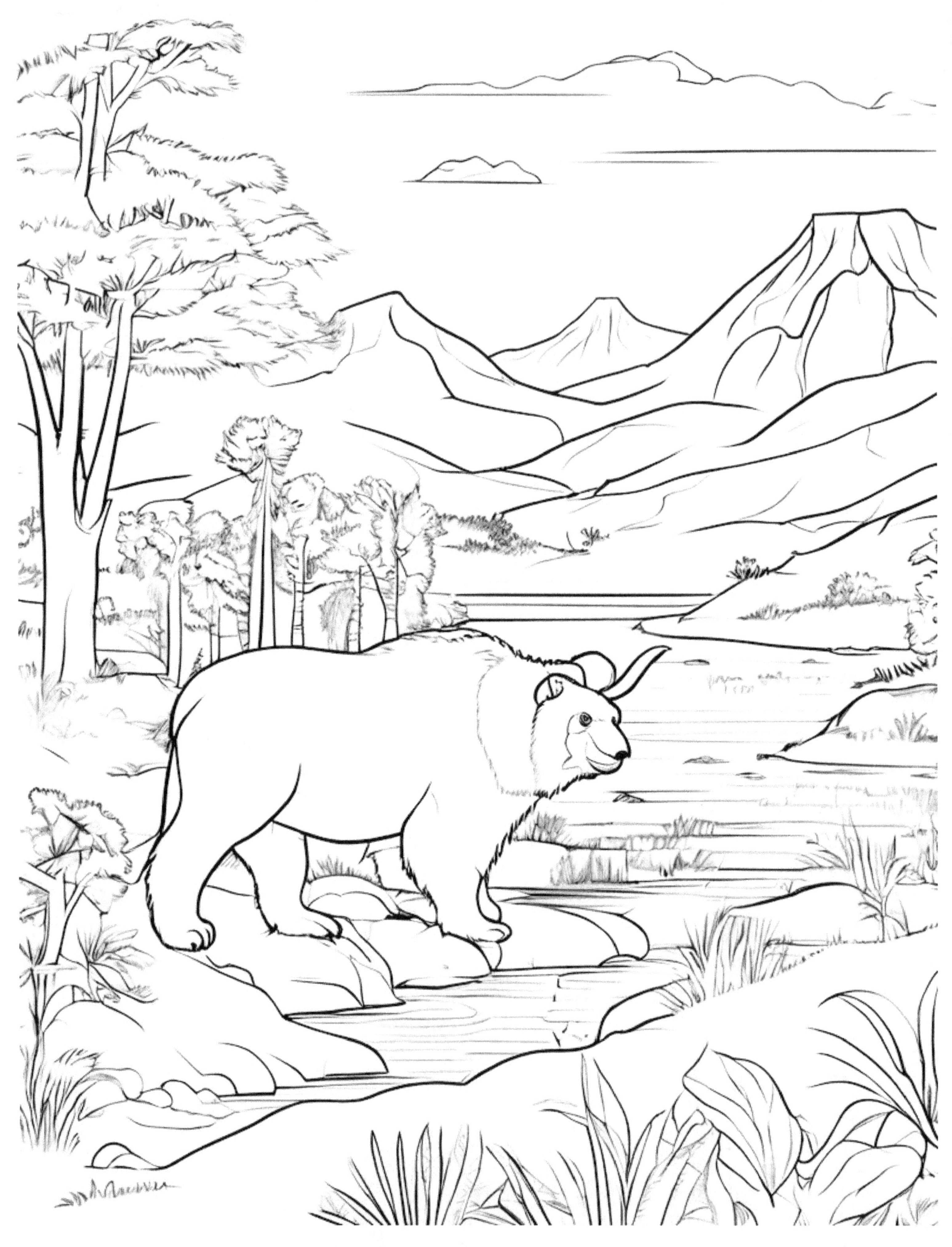

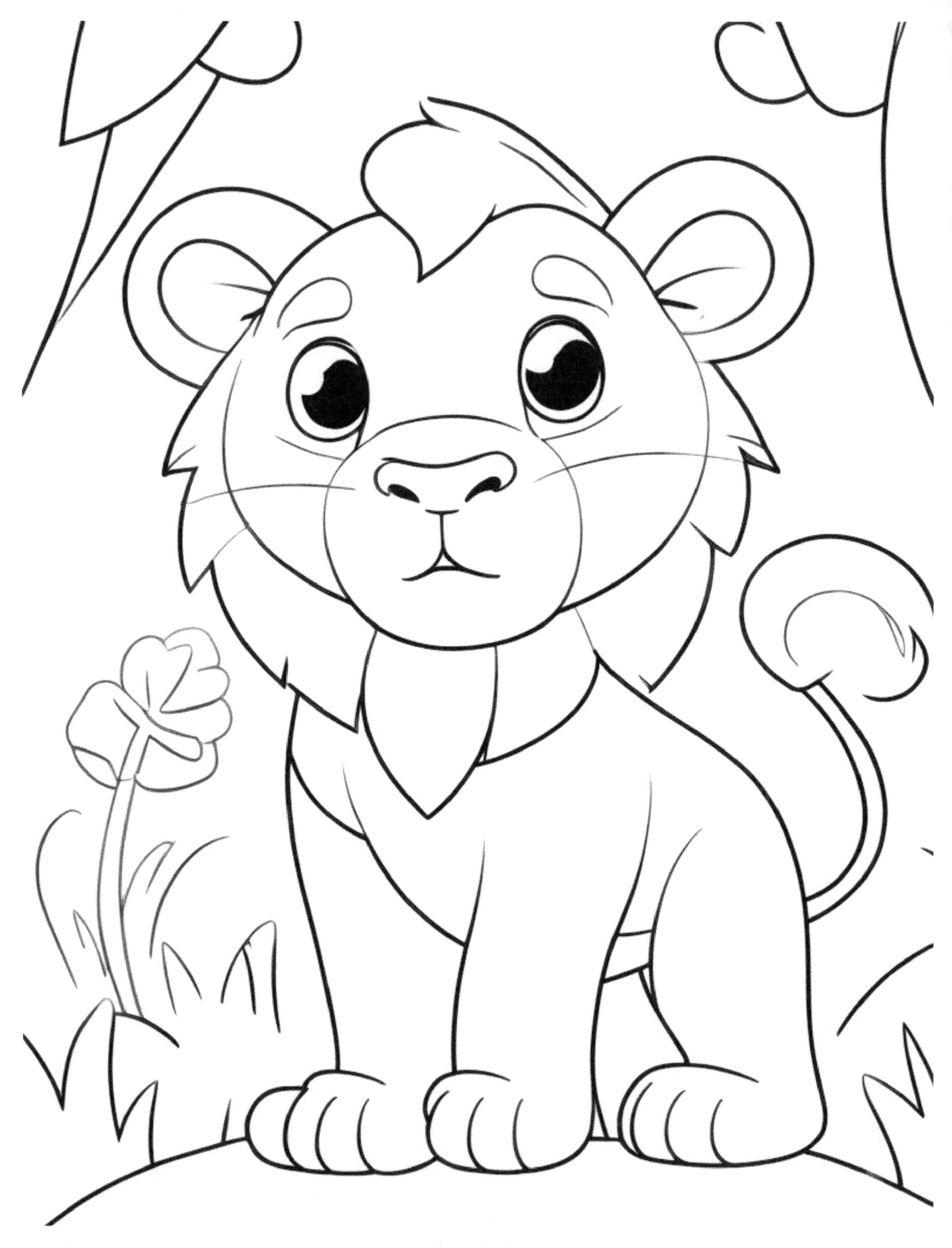

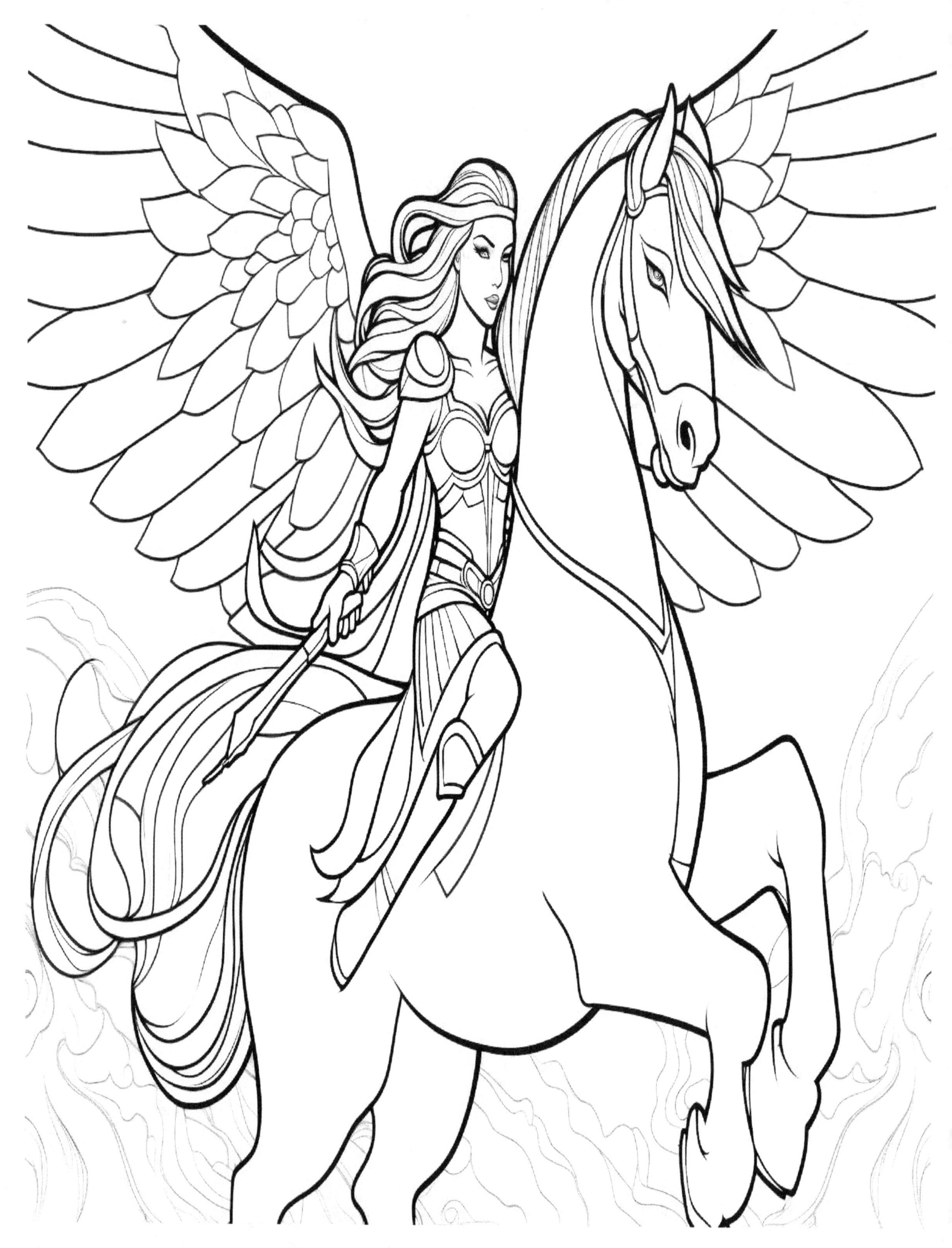